THE
ESSENCE OF
TALMUDIC LAW
AND THOUGHT

THE
ESSENCE OF
TALMUDIC LAW
AND THOUGHT

SAMUEL N. HOENIG

JASON ARONSON INC.
Northvale, New Jersey
London

The author gratefully acknowledges permission to quote from the following sources:

From *Collected Poems of Philip M. Raskin*, pp. 113-114. Copyright © 1951 by Gittel Raskin. Used by permission of Bloch Publishing Company.

From the *Treatise Ta'anit* by Henry Malter, pp. 304, 306, 334, 336, 338. Copyright © 1967 by the Jewish Publication Society of America. Used by permission of the Jewish Publication Society of America.

From *The Book of Tradition* (*Sefer ha-Qabbalah*) by Abraham ibn Daud, translated by Gershon D. Cohen, pp. 63-66. Copyright © 1967 by the Jewish Publication Society of America. Used by permission of the Jewish Publication Society of America.

From *The Essential Talmud* by Adin Steinsaltz. Copyright © 1976 by Bantam, a division of Bantam Doubleday Dell Publishing Group, Inc. Used by permission of Bantam Books, a division of Bantam Doubleday Dell Publishing Group, Inc.

From *The Earth Is the Lord's* by Abraham Joshua Heschel. Copyright © 1949 by Abraham Joshua Heschel. Copyright renewed © 1977 by Sylvia Heschel. Reprinted by permission of Farrar, Straus, & Giroux, Inc.

This book was set in 11 pt. Bem by Lind Graphics of Upper Saddle River, New Jersey.

Library of Congress Cataloging-in-Publication Data

Hoenig, Samuel N.
    The essence of talmudic law and thought / Samuel N. Hoenig.
      p. cm.
    Includes bibliographical references and index.
    ISBN 0-87668-445-2
    1. Talmud—Introductions.   2. Title.
BM503.5.H63   1993
296.1'2061—dc20

                        92-39640

Manufactured in the United States of America. Jason Aronson Inc. offers books and cassettes. For information and catalog write to Jason Aronson Inc., 230 Livingston Street, Northvale, New Jersey 07647.

CONTENTS

PREFACE

Recent times have witnessed a renewed interest in the study of Judaism. For whatever reason, there has been an upsurge on the part of Jew and non-Jew alike to search out the essence of Jewish life and thought.

The serious study of Judaism has found a prominent and legitimate place in the ivy halls of academia. No longer are courses of Jewish content tucked away in departments of Religion, Semitics, and Oriental Studies. Judaic Studies is now taught as Judaic Studies. Apologetics and the study of Judaism as background for New Testament study is by and large a thing of the past.

Coupled with this renaissance of sorts has been a proliferation of books and studies dealing with various aspects of Jewish life and literature, the Talmud being no exception.

The Essence of Talmudic Law and Thought attempts to lay before the reader the essence of talmudic thought and law. It is a story of the unfolding and making of the Talmud—its composition, structure, and redaction. Needless to say, no single work can tell the whole story of the Talmud. Its breadth and depth are so vast, its hidden treasures and insights so profound, that only the study of the Talmud itself can do it justice.

The Talmud does not contain an introduction. In fact, in Jewish tradition it is said that there is no beginning and no end to the Talmud. However, for pedagogic purposes, scholars and talmudists of the past, especially of the Geonic and Spanish medieval schools, have written introductory works to the Talmud. It is in this spirit that *The Essence of Talmudic Law and Thought* was composed.

The bulk of the sources consulted in researching and writing this work are classical, traditional Jewish writings. However, on occasion other works have been cited, true to the spirit of Maimonides, who maintains that any truthful and proven statement, regardless of its source, may be utilized in order to better our understanding of the Torah.

This work on the Talmud was originally undertaken as a thirteen-part lecture series for the Jewish People's University of the Air, a division of Touro College, under the direction of Dr. Jacob Katzman.

In the course of researching and preparing this work, I was privileged to have enjoyed the guidance, encouragement, and cooperation of many. I am grateful to Dr. Katzman for his advice and aid throughout this project. Special thanks to my brother, Mr. D. Bernard Hoenig, for his invaluable insights, stylistic suggestions, and constant encouragement. To my wife, Nechama, whose eye for perfection and pursuit of intellectual honesty serves as a model of genuine scholarship, I am eternally indebted. To my son Yosef, who in the course of "learning" together has helped me put certain issues and concepts into sharper focus, I owe a special thanks.

The book is dedicated to the memory of my dear parents, whose boundless love, devotion, and encouragement over the years have been a constant source of inspiration and happiness to me.

INTRODUCTION

The impact of talmudic thought on all of Jewish life throughout the ages is immeasurable. In a sense, the world of the Talmud is identical to the world of Judaism. To become truly familiar with the world of the Talmud, one should experience it firsthand and become fully absorbed in its study. As many sociologists maintain, the preferred approach to the study of a culture is not from an external or outside viewing. The participant-observer approach, where the observer personally becomes an active participant, is regarded as far superior. In this way one can feel the pulse of the subject and experience its very existence.

However, the study of talmudic literature is no simple task. It is not sufficient to simply read the Talmud. Indeed, one does not "read" but "studies" the Talmud. In common usage, the Yiddish word is *lernen,* to learn. One learns the Talmud. True talmudic scholars devote themselves to its pursuit with total commitment.

In our analysis of the world of the Talmud, we will not be studying Talmud per se, although our views, opinions, and conclusions are based on actual talmudic and related texts and are rooted in talmudic Jewish life. As the title of this work indicates, we shall be dealing with the "world" of the Talmud rather than with the actual talmudic texts.

WHAT EXACTLY IS THE TALMUD?

To enable us to fully understand that world, we should first define the term *Talmud*.

Talmud is derived from the Hebrew and literally means study or learning. The rabbinic literature of the Talmud is just that—a body of learning or teaching. The Talmud is also commonly referred to as *Gemara*. This is an Aramaic word that means completion or tradition. It is also sometimes called *Shas,* which consists of the initials of the words *Shishah Sedarim*—six orders—a reference to the six divisions of the *Mishnah,* the basic text of discussion in the Talmud.

Actually, there are two distinct works of Talmud: one is the Jerusalem or Palestinian Talmud, the other, the Babylonian Talmud. The Babylonian Talmud—the more popular of the two—consists of thirty-seven tractates *(massekhtot),*[1] and it is generally printed in twenty folio volumes; the total number of folio pages is 5,894. However, within the pages of the Babylonian Talmud lies much more than simply a corpus of learning. Adin Steinsaltz states:

> The Talmud is the repository of thousands of years of Jewish wisdom. And the Oral Law, which is as ancient and significant as the Written Law (the Torah), finds expression therein. It is a conglomerate of law, legend, and philosophy, a blend of unique logic and shrewd pragmatism, of history and science, anecdotes and humor.[2]

Actually, any definition of *Talmud* is beset with difficulties. As Steinsaltz further points out, the Talmud is a collection of paradoxes. On the one hand, its framework is logical and orderly, while on the other hand, "it is still based on free association, on a harnessing together of diverse ideas reminiscent of the modern stream-of-consciousness novel."[3]

Although the central purpose of the Talmud is that of legal interpretation and commentary, it nevertheless is a work of art going far beyond legislation. Furthermore, despite the fact that the Talmud is the primary source of Jewish law, it cannot be cited as an authority for purposes of ruling.[4] For these and other reasons, one scholar concludes that it is impossible to answer the question, what is the Talmud? "It is easier to say what the Talmud is not than what it is."[5]

1

HISTORICAL SETTING

The period of the Talmud involves two distinct Jewish communities—that of *Eretz Yisrael* (the land of Israel—from the time of the Restoration, 444 B.C.E., until the close of the Jerusalem Talmud, c. 350 C.E.) and the Babylonian Jewish community (from 597 B.C.E. until c. 500 C.E.).

THE CHAIN OF TRADITION AND THE TRANSMISSION OF THE ORAL LAW

Together with the Written Law, there also existed a vast body of Oral Law consisting of commentaries, expositions, and interpretations. Prior to the destruction of the First Temple in the year 586 B.C.E., the teaching and custodianship of the Oral Law was in the hands of the prophets and priests. However, during the period of Restoration, when the land of Israel was under Persian rule, a serious change took place with the return of Ezra to the Jewish homeland. The responsibilities of teaching and of religious leadership now rested in the hands of

3

a select group of scholars called *sofrim* (scribes).[1] They are also referred to as Men of the Great Assembly.[2]

Although there is a scarcity of information about the *sofrim* and, in general, the period is cloaked in obscurity, we do know that the *sofrim* left their mark upon Jewish tradition. This was especially true in three areas.

First, there was the democratization of Jewish education. The *sofrim* attempted to make the Torah the possession of all Jews rather than only of an elitist group of priests. They went about this by establishing schools of higher learning that catered to many students and not just to a select few.[3] Of special importance was the educational methodology introduced by the *sofrim*. This mode of learning, called *midrash*,[4] where the teaching of the Written Law is fused together with the Oral Law, was later to become an important component of talmudic learning.

The second contribution of the *sofrim* was their expansion and standardization of the liturgy. In former generations there existed no standard liturgy; each person chose his own text and prayed at his own convenience. The Men of the Great Assembly established a standard text, known as the *Shemoneh Esrai* or *Amidah* prayer. This consisted of eighteen benedictions, still in use today. Similarly, they expanded and introduced various other benedictions.[5]

Finally, the Men of the Great Assembly canonized the Bible. As the successors of the prophets, it was their task to redact various books of the Bible, such as Ezekiel, the Twelve Prophets, Daniel, and Esther.[6] Furthermore, they determined which books should be canonized as part of the Holy Writings or Bible.[7] The threefold division of the Jewish Bible into *Torah* (Pentateuch—the Five Books of Moses), *Nevi'im* (Prophets), and *Ketuvim* (Hagiographa or Writings) is also attributed to the *sofrim*.[8] All together they form the Hebrew Bible, the *Tanach;* the word *Tanach* is an acronym deriving from the initials of the three sections—*Torah, Nevi'im,* and *Ketuvim.*

The relative calmness of the Persian (Restoration) period was soon to give way to the turbulence of the Greek occupation of Palestine. For over a century, *Eretz Yisrael* was the battlefield of the rival warring armies of the Ptolemies and Seleucids. As a result, the Jewish homeland was not only politically and economically torn apart, but it was spiritually disintegrated as well.

During those trying times, when the zealous Seleucids disseminated Hellenic culture among their subjects, Jewish religious leadership was in the hands of the *Zugot*. The term *Zugot* (literally, "pairs"), refers to the two heads of the Sanhedrin, or High Court. The Sanhedrin functioned as a legislative body and interpreter of Jewish law, in addition to serving as a legal forum for all kinds of litigation. At the head of the Sanhedrin was the *nasi* (president), and second to him was the *av bet-din* ("father of the court"). For a brief period of about two hundred years, these *Zugot* were the spiritual guides of Jewish life and the transmitters of the Oral Law.[9]

THREE PHILOSOPHIC SECTS

During the period of the *Zugot,* between 165 B.C.E. and 37 B.C.E., when Judea had regained its independence at the hands of the heroic Maccabees, different sects emerged within Judaism. Josephus, the Jewish historian of the Second-Temple period, lists three philosophic sects: the Essenes, the Sadducees, and the Pharisees.[10]

There are various theories concerning the origin of the name *Essene*. According to one view, the name is derived from the Aramaic *asa* (to heal).[11] The Essenes, or healers, were an ascetic religious brotherhood. Their strict way of life was aimed at the attainment of *kedushah* (holiness) through the healing of all sickness caused by the sinful passions of man. They separated themselves from society and went to live in the

Judean wilderness. Wearing white linen garments, bathing in cold water, and eating in total silence were some of the more visible practices of this sect.[12] Most modern scholars identify the Qumran community as Essene and the Dead Sea Scrolls as their work.[13]

The second group mentioned by Josephus is that of the Sadducees. This sect was composed mainly of wealthy, aristocratic families. In many cases they were totally hellenized descendants of the high priest Zadok. They refused to recognize the Oral Law, or *halakhah,* as being of divine origin, and they favored a theocratic state.[14]

The third group, the Pharisees, held that the Oral Law and the Written Law were of divine origin, and they tended toward a more democratic form of government. By the first century of the present era, the Pharisees gained popularity and came to represent the religious practices, beliefs, and social outlook of the majority of the Jewish people. It was due to Pharisaic effort that a universal system of education was instituted[15] and the status of women in Judaism was elevated.[16] They remained faithful to the teachings of the *Zugot* and the Men of the Great Assembly, and they had great influence among the Jewish masses.[17]

In the year 63 B.C.E., due to inner political struggle, Judea was to lose its sovereignty to Pompeius of Rome. The despot Herod ruled as a vassal of August Caesar. He was followed by the Roman procurators, and this led to the destruction of the Temple and of the Jewish State in the year 70 C.E.

THE DESTRUCTION OF THE SECOND TEMPLE AND THE RENEWAL OF JEWISH INTELLECTUAL LIFE AT YAVNE

Tannaim is the name given to the group of rabbinic sages from the time of Hillel, one of the last of the *Zugot,* until the completion of the *Mishnah* (a compilation of the Oral Law) in the second century C.E. The term *tannaim* is from the Aramaic word *teni* (to teach, to study). The *tannaim* were both scholars and teachers. With the destruction of the Temple, the *tannaim*—members of the Pharisaic party—were intent upon revitalizing Jewish religious life. Unlike the Sadducees, they maintained that the destruction of the Temple and of the Jewish State were not the end of Judaism. They held that belief in God and observance of the Torah are timeless and know no bounds.

Under the dynamic leadership of Rabbi Yohanan ben Zakkai, a renewal of Jewish life and learning was attempted. According to an aggadic account, when he saw that Jerusalem was doomed to destruction, Rabbi Yohanan simulated death and had himself carried out of the besieged city in a coffin. Once outside the gates of the city, he went to the Roman general Vespasian and requested permission to settle in the town of Yavne with his students. The general granted Rabbi Yohanan his request.[18] The great sage set about at once to build Yavne into a spiritual center, with the Sanhedrin as its focal point. The legal, ethical, and religious teachings of the *tannaim* were later to be recorded in the *Mishnah* and other tannaitic writings.[19]

THE *AMORAIM* OF *ERETZ YISRAEL*

With the compilation of the *Mishnah,* the tannaitic period came to a close. Despite difficult times, the post-*Mishnah* scholars—referred to as *amoraim* (speakers or interpreters)—held fast to the traditions of their predecessors. In the various academies or *yeshivot,* generally located in the Galilee, the *Mishnah* was studied and expanded. In the fourth century, Christianity became the official religion of the Roman Empire, and the stability of Jewish life in Palestine was severely threatened. During the short reign of Julian the Apostate, from 360 to 363, Jewish hopes were raised. Julian attempted to revive Hellenism by diminishing the image of Christianity in the empire. Julian promised the Jewish community that he would rebuild the Temple at Jerusalem and restore the sacrificial order. He also revoked the special taxes on Jews. However, with Julian's death on the Persian front, Christians began retaliating by attacking Jewish settlements.[20] During these trying times, the *amoraim* of *Eretz Yisrael* managed to compile and edit their teachings into what is commonly known as the Jerusalem (or Palestinian) Talmud.

THE BABYLONIAN JEWISH COMMUNITY

The roots of Babylonian Jewry go back to the first captivity in the year 597 B.C.E. by Nebuchadnezzar. About ten thousand captives were taken from the land of Israel, including the king, the queen-mother, princes, warriors, craftsmen, prophets, and priests—an elitist group.[21] With the destruction of the Temple eleven years later,[22] the exiled Judeans turned to the prophets and scholars for guidance. The latter stressed the universality of the Torah.

In 537 B.C.E., with the rise of the Persian Empire, Cyrus issued his famous edict granting the Jews of Babylonia the right of return to the land of Israel.[23] But, as the historian Josephus points out, inasmuch as the Jews in Babylonia lived quite well, they were not willing to leave their wealth and possessions, and they chose to remain in exile[24]—a phenomenon that was to have its echo in our day.

Babylonia was soon to change hands; this time the Parthians seized control.[25] Under Parthian rule, the Jews of Babylonia were given the power of self-rule and were governed by their own leader, the *Resh Galuta* (Exilarch).[26] The Exilarch was a political leader serving as liaison between the Jewish community and the ruling power. During the second century, the office of Exilarch developed into a powerful instrument of government. It was even empowered to inflict the death pen-

alty and to enforce its ruling with military force when necessary.[27]

Jacob Neusner, in summarizing Jewish life in Babylonia
under Parthian rule, states:

> So the nearly four centuries of Parthian rule of Babylonia marked
> a period of security for the local Jewry. Never in that period did
> the Parthian government attempt to extirpate Judaism or to per-
> secute Jews because of their loyalty to the Judaic tradition. Reli-
> gious persecution simply did not fit into the Parthian scheme for
> governing their empire.[28]

As we have seen, the center of tannaitic activity was in *Eretz
Yisrael*. Even so, the Babylonian Jewish community was not
devoid of Torah scholars and centers of learning. Even during
this relatively early period, the Jewish community of Babylonia contained academies of learning whose scholars were in
close contact with their *Eretz Yisrael* colleagues.[29] Aside from
Hillel ha-Bavli, one of the greatest of the *tannaim* of the
Second-Temple period, we know of a number of other outstanding Babylonian *tannaim,* such as Rabbi Yehudah ben
Betara,[30] Nehemiah of Deli,[31] and Hannaiah.[32] During the
waves of Roman persecution in *Eretz Yisrael,* Babylonian
Jewry saw many scholars from that land find refuge and a
haven within its ranks.[33]

THE BABYLONIAN ACADEMIES

The zenith of Torah learning in Babylonia was reached during
the period of the *amoraim*. Under the relative calmness and
tolerance of Sassanian rule, Babylonia emerged as the center of
Torah scholarship. *Yeshivot,* academies of learning, were established in Nehardea, Sura, Pumbedita, and Mehoza. At these
academies, mature scholars gathered and, under the guidance
of the *rosh yeshivah* (dean), would analyze and elucidate, debate
and discuss Bible, *Mishnah,* and related texts.

Yarhei Kallah

An interesting innovation of the Babylonian academies was the *Yarhei Kallah* (Months of *Kallah*).[34] In normal usage, the word *kallah* means bride or betrothed, but its meaning in connection with the Months of *Kallah* is not clear.[35] At any rate, only a small percentage of the student body were able to attend the academies full-time. The majority of the students were obliged to earn their own living and therefore could attend the academy on only a part-time basis. So that a wider student body would be able to participate in the academic learning, two months of the year (*Adar* and *Elul*—roughly in March and September, off-months in farming) were therefore set aside for an intensive learning program.[36] At each *Kallah* session a different part of the *Mishnah* was studied. The *Kallah* tractate, as it was called, was determined and announced by the head of the academy at the end of the previous *Kallah,* thereby enabling the student to carry on his studies at home and thus be better prepared for the forthcoming session. During the *Kallah* months, the head of the academy lectured on that tractate and would reply to students' questions. The various types of lectures and discourses delivered at the academies eventually developed into what is called *Gemara,* or Talmud.

During the second half of the fifth century, talmudic activity began to fall off due to waves of persecution. The Babylonian Talmud was compiled, edited, and completed in about 500 C.E.

The period following that of the Talmud is known as the saboraic era. Though the saboraic period only lasted for about two hundred years, its significance for the Babylonian Talmud is important. It was during this time that the finishing touches and final editing of the Talmud were carried out.[37]

2
The Oral Law

A viable system of law must not sacrifice either its spirit or its letter. Hasty compromises, unfounded alterations, and whimsical abandonment of legal traditions lead only to chaos. Yet, in order for a legal system to endure and flourish, it is necessary that the law be flexible, elastic, and fluid, as well as definitive, clear, and steadfast.

One device that enables legal systems to remain fixed yet viable is the institution of an Oral Law. Like other systems of jurisprudence, Jewish law too has an Oral Law. In fact, when one speaks of Torah, it is necessary to distinguish between *Torah she-Bekhtav* (the Written Law) and *Torah she-Ba-al Peh* (the Oral Law).[1]

The Written Law consists of the books of the Bible, in particular, the Five Books of Moses or Pentateuch. Most basic to Judaism is the belief in the revelation at Mount Sinai—the belief that, through Moses, God revealed His will to Israel in the form of laws and precepts. These laws, or *mitzvot,* which are the essence of the Pentateuch, were to become the written possession of Israel.

THE ORAL LAW AND ITS CENTRALITY

However, the divine revelation at Sinai did not consist only of the Written Law. According to Jewish tradition, an Oral Law, both complementary and supplementary to the Written Torah, was likewise revealed to Moses at Sinai.[2] The unwritten law was transmitted orally from generation to generation.

In fact, some scholars view the Oral Law as central and as having actually preceded the Written Torah. The nineteenth-century German Jewish thinker and exegete Samson Raphael Hirsch put it this way:

> The *Torah she-Bechtav* is to be to the *Torah she-Ba'al Peh* in the relation of short notes on a full and extensive lecture on any scientific subject. For the student who has heard the whole lecture, short notes are quite sufficient to bring back afresh to his mind at any time the whole subject of the lecture. For him, a word, an added mark of interrogation, or exclamation, a dot, the underlining of a word, etc., etc., is often quite sufficient to recall to his mind a whole series of thoughts, a remark, etc. For those who had not heard the lecture from the Master, such notes would be completely useless. If they were to try to reconstruct the scientific contents of the lecture literally from such notes they would of necessity make many errors.[3]

Hirsch, in comparing the Written Torah with cryptic lecture notes and the Oral Torah to the lecture itself, is suggesting that the law, in its completeness, is not found in the Written Torah. Rather, the totality of the law can be seen only through the Oral Torah. It is the Oral Torah that is so basic and central to the Jewish scheme of jurisprudence.

The literature of the Talmud is an important part of the Oral Law. Not only has the Talmud preserved the interpretations and traditions of the Oral Law, but it is itself a link in the chain of oral tradition and a living testimony to the viability of Jewish law.

ORAL LAW AND WRITTEN LAW

A careful reading of the Pentateuch makes it clear that it was being transmitted side by side with an oral tradition. Many terms and expressions used in the Written Law are undefined. For example, Exodus 20:10 states, "The seventh day is the Sabbath of the Lord your God; in it you shall do no labor." But what is the meaning and definition of *labor?* The refraining from engaging in work on the Sabbath is most primary in Judaism. Yet, a clear-cut definition of the term *labor* is not to be found in the Written Torah. The same is true of Leviticus 23:42: "You shall dwell in booths seven days." How does one define *booths?*

Furthermore, certain passages in the Pentateuch are indeed contradictory. In Deuteronomy 23:16 we read, "The fathers shall not be put to death for the children, neither shall the children be put to death for the fathers; every man shall be put to death for his own sin." Yet, in the Ten Commandments it is stated, "For I the Lord your God am a jealous God, visiting the iniquity of the fathers upon the children unto the third and fourth generation of them that hate Me."[4] Similarly, many fundamental concepts and institutions, such as *shehitah,* ritual slaughter, divorce, and the rights of the firstborn, are all assumed by the text but not elaborated on. All of these cases indicate the reliance upon some interpretative or Oral Law.

In addition, the Pentateuch, in the Book of Deuteronomy, speaks of the authority of the Oral Law in terms of the court's interpretive and legislative powers:

> If there be a thing too hard for you in judgment, between blood and blood, between plea and plea, and between stroke and stroke, being words of strife within your gates; then you shall arise, and go up into the place which the Eternal your God shall choose; and you shall come unto the priests the Levites, and unto the judge that shall be in those days, and inquire; and they shall tell you the

words of judgment. And you shall do according to the words. . . .
And you shall observe to do according to all that they teach
you . . . you shall not depart from the word which they shall tell
you, to the right nor to the left.[5]

Thus, it is the mandate of the judges that when they are
confronted with an unprecedented situation, they rule according to oral interpretation. Such legislation is legally
binding even though no such ruling is to be found explicitly in
the Written Torah.

SINAITIC AND NON-SINAITIC LAWS

Moses Maimonides, the well-known medieval Jewish philosopher and talmudist, writing in the introduction to his *Mishnah* commentary,[6] draws a clear distinction between two types
of law—those of Sinaitic origin, that is, those that were revealed to Moses at Sinai, and those of non-Sinaitic origin.
    Laws originating and received by Moses at Sinai fall into
two categories. At Sinai, together with the Written Torah,
various interpretations of Scripture were revealed to Moses.
These explanations were given orally, and they were transmitted from generation to generation, eventually finding their
way into the Talmud and *midrash*. Though these interpretations are outside of the written text, they are somehow indicated in the text and can be extracted from it, by means of text
analysis. For example, on the festival of Sukkot we are commanded to take an *etrog* (citron).[7] Nevertheless, the term *etrog* is
not to be found in the text of the Pentateuch. The biblical text
reads simply, "And you shall take unto you on the first day the
fruit of goodly trees."[8] What precisely is the meaning of "fruit
of goodly trees"? Is it an apple, a pomegranate, or perhaps a
quince? From earliest times, "fruit of goodly trees" meant

etrog.[9] Therefore, such an interpretation is considered a Sinaitic (orally transmitted) explanation of the text, that "fruit of a goodly tree" is identified as the *etrog*.

Though this type of exegesis is of a revealed or Sinaitic nature, the talmudic sages nevertheless produced scriptural proof for such explanations. Concerning the case at hand, pointing to the Hebrew term employed by the text for "goodly" (*hadar,* which when accented differently means *ha-dor,* "to dwell"), the rabbis found a proof text for the oral tradition concerning the *etrog*. The text refers to a fruit that stays on the tree from year to year, and this is none other than the *etrog*![10] Laws belonging to this group are not subject to challenge, nor may they be revoked at a later time.

The second category of Sinaitic laws mentioned by Maimonides are those laws, given to Moses, that have no intrinsic connection with the Written Law.[11] Some examples of this are the requirement of black straps for *tefillin* (phylacteries) and the minimum dimensions of food for the recital of blessings.[12] Any attempt to extract such laws from the written text is baseless, for such laws are totally independent of the Written Torah. These laws, too, are not subject to revocation or challenge.

More complex are the oral laws of non-Sinaitic origin. According to Maimonides, the first type of laws that belong to this category are those that are based upon logic and reason. By applying logic, or hermeneutical principles, to the text of the Written Torah, the rabbis created new laws.[13]

METHODS OF *DERASH*

The Bible authorizes the judges and sages to interpret and derive laws from the Torah. Inasmuch as the rabbis are interpreting, either logically or by means of *derash* (that is, by deriving *halakhah* from the biblical texts themselves and not legislating completely new laws), these newly created interpretations are considered of biblical status.[14] For example, one is forbidden to kill another individual in order to save one's own life. Though such a law is not to be found anywhere in the Written Torah, it is considered biblical, not rabbinic law! The source for this law is logic. As the Talmud points out, "Who told you that your blood is redder than his,"[15] or in other words, why should you live at the expense of another's life? Thus, the talmudic sages are not creating or legislating a completely new law. They are merely interpreting Exodus 20:13, which says, "You shall not murder," and stating that logically, killing an innocent person to save your own life is included in "You shall not murder." By resorting to *derash,* the rabbis here engaged in a creative-interpretive process.

Concerning the talmudic usage of *derash,* whether it be of the creative-interpretive type or of the proof text category, the following legend is related:

When Moses ascended on high he found the Holy One, blessed be He, engaged in affixing coronets to the letters of the Torah. Said Moses, "Lord of the Universe, who stays Thy hand?" He answered, "There will arise a man, at the end of many generations, Akiva ben Yosef by name, who will expound upon each tittle heaps and heaps of laws." "Lord of the Universe," said Moses; "permit me to see him." He replied, "Turn around." Moses went and sat down behind eight rows (and listened to the discourses upon the law). Not being able to follow their arguments he was ill at ease, but when they came to a certain subject and the disciples said to the master "Whence do you know it?" and the latter replied "It is a law given unto Moses at Sinai" he was comforted.[16]

Even Moses, the greatest of prophets, the teacher of Torah par excellence, the very recipient of the Torah, was not privy

to the text proofs or creative interpretations of Rabbi Akiva.[17]
The Torah, through its Oral Law, is an ongoing learning
process of dynamic proportion. In no small degree, the great
rabbinic scholars of all ages contribute and lend credence to the
viability of the *halakhah*.

In most cases it is difficult to ascertain whether a *derash* is of
the proof text or creative-interpretive type. In fact, the noted
Jewish historian Isaac Halevi is of the opinion that the creative
derash was very rare, and in any event is limited only to the
Great Sanhedrin of Jerusalem.[18]

LAWS OF RABBINIC ORIGIN

The final division of the Oral Law comprises those laws
created by rabbinic legislation.[19] There are two types of rabbinic enactment or legislation. The first kind of legislative laws
is called *gezerot* (decrees). Such laws were established to safeguard the Torah, or as the rabbis themselves put it, "to create
a fence around the laws of the Torah."[20] Cognizant of human
weaknesses, the sages attempted to limit temptation by enacting "preventive legislation." Precedent for laws of this type
is found in the Bible. Take, for example, the case of the
Nazarite. Although forbidden to drink wine, the Bible nevertheless instructs the Nazarite to abstain from everything related to the vine: "He must separate himself completely from
the wine and wine-brandy. He may not even drink vinegar
made from wine and wine-brandy. He shall not drink any
beverage, and he shall not eat any grapes or raisins."[21] All
these extra precautionary measures were taken in order to
forestall violation of the biblical injunction against the Nazarite's drinking of wine.

The rabbis of the Talmud, taking their cue from the Bible,
expanded this type of legislation to other areas where and

when necessary.[22] Various *gezerot* were decreed concerning the observance of the Sabbath, the dietary laws, and matters of sexual morality. The *gezerah* was of such importance that in certain instances it even superseded a positive commandment of the Torah. Thus, the *shofar* (ram's horn) is not sounded on the holy day of Rosh Hashanah, the Jewish New Year, when it occurs on a Sabbath, in order to avoid possible violation of a Sabbath ordinance.[23]

Once a *gezerah* is legislated and has become widespread among the Jewish people, it can never be repealed. Even if a *gezerah* were to become inapplicable and obsolete, it could not be rescinded by a later rabbinic legislative body.[24] To avoid this type of situation, certain *gezerot* were enacted only for prevailing conditions and circumstances. When those conditions no longer existed, the decree automatically became null and void. An example of this is the rabbinic decree against drinking uncovered water.[25] This *gezerah* was made in a time and in countries where snakes were common, and consequently it was never intended for other lands or times.

Unlike the *gezerah* type of legislation is the *takanah* (ordinance). In order to improve compliance with religious law or cope with new situations, the rabbis throughout the ages have legislated *takanot*. *Takanot* cover the spectrum of law and life, ranging from the protection of a divorced or widowed woman to the enactment of various prayers and benedictions.

When the Second Temple was destroyed in 70 C.E., there was great concern about the future of Jewish observance and tradition. To cope with this "new" situation, a series of *takanot* were passed by the sages. These legislative measures attempted to rebuild Jewish life while retaining a remembrance of the Temple. Thus, in an ancient rabbinic text we read, "Originally the *lulav* (palm branch used during the Sukkot festival) was used for seven days in the Temple and for one day elsewhere. When the Temple was destroyed, Rabbi Yohanan ben Zakkai ruled that the *lulav* should be used everywhere for seven days, in memory of the Temple."[26]

MINHAG: CUSTOM

Also part of rabbinic law is the *minhag,* or local custom. In matters of halakhic dispute, often a community would accept one opinion over another. In the course of time, this gave rise to different halakhic practices, such as those of the Ashkenazim and the Sephardim. Great stress was placed on the importance of respecting and conforming to local custom: Rabbi Tanhum said, "Never should a person differ from the local custom, for did not Moses refrain from eating when he ascended to heaven in deference to the angels whose custom it is not to eat? And did not the angels eat when they descended to earth to visit Abraham?"[27]

This reverence and respect shown to local custom is further seen from the following story:

> The citizens of Beyshan (a village in Lebanon) were accustomed not to go from Tyre to Sidon on the eve of the Sabbath (to sell their goods). Their children went to Rabbi Yohanan and said to him: For our fathers this was possible; for us it is impossible. Rabbi Yohanan thereupon replied: Your fathers have already taken it upon themselves once and for all.[28]

In this talmudic account, though the children, unlike their parents, could not afford to miss Friday's market day, nevertheless the *minhag* (custom of the fathers) prevailed. In this instance the *minhag* takes on a religious quality; it becomes part of *halakhah* and cannot be terminated simply because its observance has become more difficult due to financial reasons.

Of special interest is the question of whether *minhag,* like rabbinic decrees *(gezerot)* and ordinances *(takanot),* is capable of setting aside and overriding the law. Generally speaking, the principle that "custom overrides the law"[29] is applicable only to matters of civil law. Jewish civil law, unlike ritual precepts and observances, is subject to contract, convention, and stipulation. This means that Jewish civil law is binding only as long as the involved parties do not disclose their preference for another arrangement. Ritual law, on the other hand, is not subject to the will of the involved parties. Thus, matters of civil law give rise to a more flexible attitude toward the prevailing custom, even when contradicting the generally accepted law.[30]

It must be remembered, however, that *minhag,* as a true expression of the Oral Law, must reflect a genuine Torah point of view. Joseph Kalir, writing on the subject of *minhag,* states:

> Only a *minhag* which can be considered an expression of the religious spirit manifest in Israel can qualify as *Minhag Yisrael* (Jewish Custom). . . . A proper *minhag* must be derived and practiced in the full knowledge of the *din* (law) itself. What has become custom through misinterpretation of the *din* can never gain binding strength.[31]

ADDING TO THE TORAH

A frequent issue concerning rabbinic legislation is that of adding to the words of the Torah. The Bible says, "You shall not add to the word which I command you."[32] Are the rabbis not adding to the Torah when legislating, decreeing, and enacting? The answer to this question lies in the difference between adding to God's laws and creating a new system of rabbinic laws. Rabbinic laws and Torah laws are two separate entities. As per the authority vested in the rabbis, they have the legislative powers to enact *takanot* and *gezerot*. So long as these *takanot* and *gezerot* are clearly identified as being of rabbinic origin, serving as a safeguard of Torah laws, the prohibition against adding to the Torah is not applicable.[33] Harry Schimmel states, "One does not add to the Empire State Building by erecting another building 102 stories high, but by increasing the height of the existing building."[34]

Though the Oral Law has now been reduced to writing in the form of the *Mishnah, midrash,* and *Gemara,* originally it was transmitted and taught in verbal form. Oral transmission is not unique to Judaism. As the American archaeologist William Foxwell Albright notes, "Writing was used in antiquity largely as an aid or guide to memory, not as a substitute for it."[35] In classical antiquity, pupils were expected to memorize Virgil and Homer; Moslem boys, even today, learn the Koran by heart; the Hindus memorize the Vedas; and not too long ago, Chinese classics were all committed to memory.

THE COMMITTING OF THE ORAL LAW TO WRITING

Concerning the Oral Law, we find a talmudic injunction against its being committed to writing.[36] Maimonides, following closely the original wording of the injunction, concludes that the prohibition against writing down the Oral Torah was only insofar as one was not to teach the Oral Law publicly from a written document. However, no injunction existed against writing down the Oral Law for private use in the form of personal notes.[37]

The *midrash* notes that Moses had requested that God give the Oral Torah in writing. God responds to Moses that the Oral Law is not given in writing in order to preserve the distinctiveness of the Jewish people. It goes on to say that the

Oral Law must remain the unique possession of Israel, thereby distinguishing them from other nations. If the Oral Law, like the Bible, had been written down from the very beginning, it too would have been taken over by others and thus would have ceased to be the singular possession of the Jewish people.[38]

3

THE LITERATURE OF
THE *TANNAIM*

It was during the period of the *tannaim*—the sages of the first and second centuries in the land of Israel—that the Oral Law began to receive a fixed literary form. The teachings of the Oral Law of this period have been preserved in two very distinct forms—the midrashic and the mishnaic arrangements.

MIDRASH AND MISHNAH

The word *midrash* is derived from the root *derash*. It means to investigate or examine, and it refers to the searching out of, or the examination of, the Written Torah. Though most of the *midrashim* are aggadic (nonlegalistic) in nature, a good number of the earlier *midrashim* are halakhic—they deal with aspects of law. The word *halakhah* is from the Hebrew *halokh* (to go), and it is used in reference to Jewish law, for it entails the approaches to the rules of Jewish living and behavior. Thus, *midrash halakhah* is basically a running commentary on the legal sections of the Pentateuch.

Most scholars of the *midrash* maintain that the midrashic form preceded the mishnaic style.[1] The mishnaic style is *halakhah* (law), presented in a form divorced from the Written Torah.

During the times of Ezra and the Men of the Great Assembly, the accepted mode of study was the midrashic style. Adin Steinsaltz describes the midrashic studies of this period:

> It was these scribes who evolved the basic methods of *midrash halakhah* (halakhic exegesis), that is, methods of learning and deriving *halakhah* from the biblical texts themselves, reconciling apparent textual contradictions, interpreting enigmatic statements, and analyzing and solving problems through perusal of the text.[2]

THE SCHOOLS OF RABBI AKIVA AND RABBI YISHMAEL

Though the *midrash* form was eventually to give way to the simpler mishnaic style, nevertheless, it was not to be completely forgotten. During the tannaitic period, in the first and second centuries of the common era, prominent tannaitic academies engaged in biblical exegesis along midrashic lines. In the schools of Rabbi Akiva and Rabbi Yishmael, special attention was given to the study of *midrash halakhah*. From these two schools were to emerge the various texts of the halakhic *midrashim*.

Though both academies engaged in midrashic exegesis, their approaches and emphases differed. George Foot Moore describes some of the differences between Rabbi Akiva and Rabbi Yishmael:

> In the interpretation of Scripture, Akiva went on the principle that in a book of divine revelation no smallest peculiarity of expression or even of spelling is accidental or devoid of significance, and

evolved certain new hermeneutic rules for the discovery of the meaning thus suggested by the letter. By these methods, and by fabulous acumen and ingenuity in the employment of them, Akiva found in the written law many things for which theretofore it had been possible only to allege to tradition. . . . Yishmael adhered more closely to the methods of interpretation embodied in the seven norms of Hillel. These he analyzed and subdivided, with some modification, into thirteen, which became the standard principles of juristic hermeneutics. In contradiction to Akiva he held that the Torah speaks ordinary human language; varieties in the mode of expression of which in common speech no notice would be taken are not to be forced to yield a hidden significance.[3]

Some scholars were able to determine the origin of the different halakhic *midrashim* that have come down to us by noting in the *midrashim* the frequency of *tannaim*'s names, or anonymous statements recorded in the *midrashim* but elsewhere attributed to Rabbi Akiva or Rabbi Yishmael, or internal factors, such as terminologies and varying hermeneutical rules.[4]

Two important points concerning the different books of *midrash* must be stressed.[5] First, though they emanate from the academies of Rabbi Akiva and Rabbi Yishmael, they also contain expositions coming from an earlier period. These early *midrashim* were preserved and handed down from generation to generation, eventually finding their way into the midrashic literature. In fact, in the opinion of one scholar, the *midrash halakhah* is a repository of passages composed as early as the Babylonian exile.[6] Second, though these midrashic works are called *midrash halakhah,* they contain an abundance of nonhalakhic or aggadic (nonlegal) material.

The essence of *midrash halakhah* can be experienced by a study of a commentary on Exodus:

You shall not steal (Exodus 20:13). Why is this said? Because it says And he that steals a man and sells him . . . he shall surely be put to death (Exodus 21:16). We have thus heard the penalty for it, but we have not heard the warning against it. Therefore it says here You shall not steal. Behold then there is a warning against stealing persons (kidnapping).

Thus far, the *midrash* has shown that the commandment "You shall not steal" refers to the more horrendous crime of kidnapping and not to the stealing of money.

The text continues:

Perhaps it is not so, but it is a warning against stealing money? When it says—You shall not steal (Leviticus 19:11), behold there you have a warning against stealing money. Hence, to what does the passage You shall not steal (Exodus 20:13) refer? To kidnapping.

The *midrash* challenges the original premise by suggesting that Exodus 20:13 alludes to the stealing of money. This, however, is rejected. Since Leviticus 19:11 speaks of stealing money, the verse in Exodus must be speaking of something else.

But the *midrash* raises the further question:

Perhaps the passage here (Exodus 20:13) is a prohibition against stealing money and the passage there (Leviticus 19:11) is a prohibition against kidnapping?

To this it answers:

You must reason: Go and learn it by one of the thirteen rules according to which the Torah is interpreted—that is, by something that is deduced from the context. What does Scripture deal with here? Crimes punishable by death. So too, we have here a crime that is punishable by death.[7]

By the hermeneutical rule that an ambiguous statement is explained from its context, the *midrash* proves that the phrase

"You shall not steal," as set forth in Exodus 20:13, is referring to kidnapping. In the case of Exodus (the Ten Commandments), the context is the other negative commandments of "You shall not murder" and "You shall not commit adultery"—both capital crimes. From this we infer that "you shall not steal" similarly speaks of a form of stealing that is punishable by death, i.e., kidnapping.

TRANSITION FROM *MIDRASH* TO *MISHNAH*: WHY AND WHEN?

As previously noted, the midrashic form eventually gave way to the mishnaic style: the presentation of *halakhah* in a form independent of the Written Torah. What brought about this change? Various theories have been advanced concerning this question. First, inasmuch as the Oral Law was not allowed to be written down, it was much easier to memorize the law itself without any scriptural references. Thus, the mishnaic form of clear, concise statements of law was preferred. A second view maintains that due to the increase of rabbinic legislation, without scriptural proof, the midrashic style became unsuitable. Another theory suggests that the mishnaic form's topical classification was superior to the midrashic style that scattered about different aspects of the same topic.[8]

Harry Schimmel offers yet another possible explanation:

> When a *halakhah* is stated to be derived from a Scriptural passage, it is open to the argument that the passage concerned has been misinterpreted. The *Mishnaic* style, on the other hand, bears the hallmark of finality and the *halakhah* is stated beyond all argument.[9]

A more basic question concerning the *Mishnah* is, when did the transition from midrashic to mishnaic form take place? The

Mishnah was edited and arranged by Rabbi Judah the Prince around 200 C.E. However, talmudic sources indicate that even before Rabbi Judah, some form of the *Mishnah* already existed. How far back the *Mishnah* form can be traced is subject to conjecture. Some maintain that the first complete arrangement of *Mishnah* dates back to the Men of the Great Assembly, that is, the early period of the Second Temple.[10] Others see the first arrangements and collections of *Mishnah* texts as taking form during the Yavnean period, following the destruction of the Second Temple. At Yavne, the *tannaim* began classifying the various *halakhot* (legal findings). This early attempt at classification of the Oral Law into *mishnayot* has remained intact, and it is found in tractate *Eduyyot* of the *Mishnah*.[11]

Regardless of when the Oral Law first began to appear in *mishnaic* form, the *Mishnah* as we know it today was compiled by Rabbi Judah the Prince. Aside from arranging and editing the vast corpus of Oral Law and the early *mishnayot,* Rabbi Judah included his own opinions on various matters as well.

THE SIX ORDERS OF THE *MISHNAH*

The *Mishnah* is written in a terse but lucid Hebrew. Its contents are divided into six orders, covering the whole spectrum of Jewish law. The six orders, or divisions, are *Zeraim* (Seeds), dealing with agricultural laws and prayers; *Moed* (Festivals), pertaining to the laws of the Sabbath and festivals; *Nashim* (Women), concerning marriage and divorce; *Nezikin* (Damages), which deals with Jewish civil and criminal law; *Kodashim* (Sacred Things), involving sacrificial rites, the Temple, and dietary laws; and *Tohorot* (Pure Things), relating to ritual and family purities.

Each of these divisions—in Hebrew they are called *sedarim* (orders)—is divided into tractates *(massekhtot).* Each *massekhta* (tractate) consists of chapters that are divided into smaller units called *mishnayot*.

It is not clear whether Rabbi Judah actually committed the *Mishnah* to writing, thereby creating a written record of the Oral Law, or simply rearranged the teachings to function as an officially approved body of law. Maimonides maintains that Rabbi Judah did in fact write down the *Mishnah,* inasmuch as the original ban against writing the Oral Law had already been lifted.[12] Others disagree. They are of the view that the *Mishnah* was not written down until the postamoraic period, that is, until the sixth century.[13]

Examining a *Mishnah* text and pointing out some of its salient features is a good introduction to the *Mishnah.* The first *Mishnah* of tractate *Berakhot, Seder Zeraim,* reads as follows:

> From when (in the evening) are we to read the *Shema* (the prayer Hear O Israel, the Lord is our God, the Lord is One)? From the moment when the priests come in to eat of their heave-offering, up to the end of the first watch. This is the opinion of Rabbi Eliezer, but the Sages say, until midnight. Rabbi Gamliel says, until dawn. . . .

This *Mishnah* is dealing with a basic halakhic issue, namely, the biblical requirement to recite the *Shema* prayer each evening. The text of the *Shema* follows Deuteronomy 6:4–9. The *Mishnah* gives us the earliest possible time to fulfill this obligation—"from the moment when the priests come in to eat of their heave-offering," which is equivalent to nightfall. As to when one may carry out this requirement, the *Mishnah* lists three opinions. Rabbi Eliezer says this requirement needs to be carried out until the end of the first watch (the night was considered twelve hours in length, divided into three watches of four hours each). The sages disagree and maintain that one has until midnight to recite the *Shema,* and Rabbi Gamliel extends the time to dawn.

THE *MISHNAH*: CODE OR COMPENDIUM?

Considering this *Mishnah* as a legal code raises some serious questions. Inasmuch as a code of law attempts to render the law certain, simple, accessible, logically arranged, and harmonious, one can only wonder how this and similar *mishnayot* are deemed a codified law. No definite rule of law is set down. Rather, three different opinions are cited. Furthermore, the *Mishnah* is obviously concerned with the exact definition of the phrase "and when you lie down." That phrase is contained in the biblical reference to the *Shema,* "And you shall discuss them when you sit in your house and when you travel on the road, and when you lie down and when you rise up." Yet, no such source is cited in the *Mishnah.* Instead of directly stating that the *Shema* may be recited beginning at nightfall, the *tanna* obliquely states that this may be "from the time when the priests may begin to eat of their heave-offering" (which happens to be at nightfall).

Indeed, the *Mishnah* in no way resembles a legal code in the modern sense. Nevertheless, many scholars insist that Rabbi Judah was concerned with codifying the law and wished to formulate the final *halakhah;* at the same time, he tried to reveal the differences and conflicts that led up to such finalization.[14]

Others feel it was not Rabbi Judah's intention to create a code of Jewish law. The *Mishnah,* they maintain, is simply a collection or compendium of the Oral Law. Without altering or changing opinions, Rabbi Judah merely recorded the teachings of the Oral Torah as received by him, adding to it the teachings of his own generation.

PUBLICATION OF THE *MISHNAH* AND RABBI JUDAH THE PRINCE

Actually, the systematic organization of the Oral Law into clearly defined units began with Rabbi Akiva (50–135 C.E.).

The activities of Rabbi Akiva with respect to the *Mishnah* are eloquently described in *Avot de-Rabbi Natan,* a supplementary tractate to *Avot (Ethics of the Fathers).* According to this, Rabbi Judah the Prince used to list the excellences of the sages:

> Rabbi Akiva he called a well-stocked storehouse. To what might Rabbi Akiva be likened? To a laborer who took his basket and went forth. When he found wheat, he put some in the basket, when he found barley, he put that in; spelt, he put that in; lentils, he put them in. Upon returning home, he sorted out the wheat by itself, the barley by itself, the beans by themselves, the lentils by themselves. This is how Rabbi Akiva acted, and he arranged the whole Torah in rings.[15]

Rabbi Akiva, the allegorical field laborer, studied and absorbed various disorganized subjects and subsequently classified them into individual units and categories.

This sort of work was continued by Rabbi Akiva's disciples. It is Rabbi Meir, one of Rabbi Akiva's most gifted students, whose system of organization and compilation served as the basis for Rabbi Judah's *Mishnah.*[16]

In his academy, Rabbi Judah the Prince scrutinized and clarified the existing texts of the Oral Law. Sometimes an ancient mishnaic formulation was left in its original form, while at other times the text underwent editorial change. In this way, Rabbi Judah served as the redactor of the *Mishnah,* and this version was accepted by all. It has remained virtually stable and unchanged to this day.

With the completion of the *Mishnah* and the death of Rabbi Judah in the year 210 C.E., the period of the *tannaim* came to a close.[17] For about a generation after Rabbi Judah's death, his young colleagues and disciples continued to engage in the compiling and editing of tannaitic source material. As Adin Steinsaltz points out, "Although it was generally agreed that his (Rabbi Judah's) codification work was the most important, it was thought worthwhile to preserve the extraneous material as an aid to study and for comparative purposes."[18]

ADDITIONAL COMPILATIONS: *TOSEFTA* AND *BARAITA*

Two of Rabbi Judah's students—Rabbi Hiya and Rabbi Oshaya—continuing in their master's footsteps, compiled additional collections of the Oral Law. One such collection is called the *Tosefta. Tosefta,* which literally means supplement or addition, is a halakhic collection of tannaitic teachings written in the mishnaic style. Like the *Mishnah,* the *Tosefta* is divided into six orders arranged into tractates *(massekhtot).* The *Tosefta* covers all tractates of the *Mishnah* with the exception of four.[19] Though the formulation of the *halakhah* in the *Tosefta* is almost identical to and sometimes overlaps that of the *Mishnah,* in many instances the *Tosefta* goes beyond the *Mishnah.* Thus, elements of *Mishnah* commentary are to be found in the *Tosefta,* while at the same time an unclear or ambiguous *Mishnah* text is elucidated upon, often in the form of a running commentary.

Also, while serving as a commentary to the *Mishnah,* the *Tosefta,* at times, deviates from Rabbi Judah's *Mishnah.* What might appear in the *Mishnah* as an undisputed ruling is subject to disagreement in the *Tosefta.* Variant readings from the *Mishnah* are quite common in the *Tosefta.* On occasion, the *Tosefta* will supply us with additional *halakhot* that are not even recorded in the *Mishnah.*[20]

In addition to the *Tosefta,* other tannaitic compilations were made during the early post-*Mishnah* transitional period. The abundance of such existing material is interestingly noted in the *midrash* in commenting upon a verse in the Song of Songs: "Threescore queens—refers to the sixty tractates of the *halakhot (Mishnah);* fourscore concubines—to the eighty sections of *Torat Kohanim;* virgins without number—to the *Toseftot.*"[21]

All such compilations and tannaitic teachings not actually included in the *Mishnah* are known as *baraitot*. This is an Aramaic word that means outside teachings, that is, outside of the canon of the *Mishnah*.

Eventually, the work of preserving, codifying, and compiling was to give way to one of explaining and expounding, of analytical, textual, and conceptual study of the *Mishnah* and *baraitot*.

4

AMORAIC LITERATURE AND THE FORMATION OF THE TALMUD

The publication of the *Mishnah* in about the year 200 C.E. brought the period of the *tannaim* to a close.[1] With the *Mishnah* at the center of Jewish rabbinic studies, generations of scholars, both in the land of Israel and in Babylonia (present-day Iraq), carefully studied and analyzed it, with emphasis on its relationship to other tannaitic teachings. The teachings of the *amoraim* (the sages and scholars who carried out this mode of study[2]) were eventually collected and compiled into the Talmud, which means teaching. The Talmud is most frequently referred to as the *Gemara*. The word *Talmud* literally means completion or tradition, and the oral tradition, as embodied in the *Gemara,* complements the Written Torah.[3]

MAIMONIDES' FOUR OBJECTIVES OF THE *GEMARA*

In his *Introduction to the Commentary on the Mishnah,* Moses Maimonides lists four main objectives of the *Gemara:*

41

1. To explain the *Mishnah* by recording the divergent opinions as to their intent, and to give the bases of the arguments of each scholar against his colleague so as to reveal the final decision.
2. To record the final decision.
3. To record the new applications that the sages of each generation derived from the *Mishnah*, disclosing the basic principles upon which the *tannaim* based their opinions; and also to record the *gezerot* and *takanot* enacted since the completion of the *Mishnah*.
4. To record the aggadic *Derashot* (nonlegal matters, such as legends, historical records, and theological and ethical teachings).[4]

Thus, the Talmud's subject matter is divided into *halakhah* (legal teachings) and the *aggadah* (nonlegal matters, such as legends, historical records, theological teachings, and ethical teachings).

THE *MEMRA* AND *SUGYAH*

To the uninitiated, the *Gemara* is like a vast, unending sea. However, there is a basic structure to this expansive work. There are essentially two basic literary units in amoraic literature: the *memra* and the *sugyah*. A *memra*, which literally means a saying, has been defined as "a short amoraic statement which contains a complete idea, without any dialectics."[5] A *memra* is usually introduced by the word *amar*—"a certain *amora* said," or *itmar*—"it has been said" or "it is reported." The second unit is called the *sugyah*. A *sugyah* is the treatment of a single topic in a dialectical form.[6] In most cases, the *memra* and the *sugyah* are related directly to the *Mishnah*, and they are usually explanatory in nature. However, there are *memrot* and *sugyot* that are wholly independent of the *Mishnah*. The *memrot* and *sugyot* originated at different times and places, and they were later strung together to form units of *Mishnah* commentary.

LOGIC AND DIALECTICS

A typical *sugyah* employs two basic methods of explication: logic and dialectics. This varies from *amora* to *amora*. It also relies on authoritative prooftexts derived from the *Mishnah, Tosefta, midrash halakhah,* and early amoraic *memrot* (sayings).[7] Within the literary unit of the *sugyah,* one may uncover many strata. In early amoraic times the *sugyah* was brief, consisting of a *memra* with only one or two questions and their answers. In subsequent generations, the rabbis would deal with a *Mishnah* by analyzing the "early" *sugyah,* adding to it their own views and opinions, queries, and solutions. Thus, a *sugyah* may very well span five or six generations of *amoraim*.

An examination of the first *Mishnah* and *Gemara* in the second chapter of tractate *Kiddushin* in the Babylonian Talmud[8] illustrates the technique of the *memra* and *sugyah.* The subject matter deals with the laws of betrothal and marriage. According to talmudic law, when a man and a woman decide to wed, it is necessary for the man to say to the woman in the presence of two acceptable witnesses that she now becomes his wife, and he must use one of the accepted modes of matrimony.[9] He may symbolically hand over some money, or something having the value of money, to her. He may give her a written document or deed for the purpose of effecting the betrothal. Or, he may have sexual intercourse with her, thereby effecting the bond of marriage. The betrothal is then followed with *nisuin,* the actual wedding, where the man brings his betrothed into his home. Today the *huppah* (canopy) is used to symbolize their new abode.

The *Mishnah* states:

A man may betroth a woman through himself or through his agent. A woman may be betrothed through herself or through her agent.[10]

According to the *Mishnah,* the symbolic handing over of money, or something having the value of money, need not be done by the groom himself. He may appoint proxies for this purpose. According to the law of agency, "a man's agent is as himself."[11]

Concerning the statement in the *Mishnah* "that a man may betroth a woman by himself or through his agent," the *Gemara* asks:

If he can betroth through his agent, is it necessary to state through himself?[12]

To this the *Gemara* replies by citing a *memra:*

Said Rabbi Joseph: This inclusion in the *Mishnah* that he can betroth through himself intimates that it is more meritorious through himself than through his agent. Even as Rabbi Safra, himself, singed an animal's head (in preparation for the Sabbath, though another could have done it for him). Similarly, Rabbah himself salted the fish called *shibuta.*[13]

Thus we can understand why the author of the *Mishnah* felt it necessary to state that a man may betroth a woman by himself as well as by proxy. Even though betrothal via an agent is legitimate, it is, nevertheless, more meritorious if the man does it himself.

The *Gemara* continues and cites another point of view:

Some say that in this matter there is even a prohibition against appointing an agent when he can do it himself, in accordance with

Rabbi Judah's dictum in Rav's name: For Rabbi Judah said in the name of Rav, a man may not betroth a woman before he sees her, lest he subsequently see something repulsive in her, and she becomes loathsome to him, whereas the All Merciful said "but you shall love your neighbor as yourself."[14]

According to the second *memra*, Rabbi Judah, in the name of Rav, maintains that a man may not betroth through an agent if he can do it himself. For this reason the *Mishnah* states that "a man may betroth through himself." Having before us two contradictory *memrot*, the *Gemara* attempts to reconcile the two:

And as to Rabbi Joseph's statement, that it is preferable that he do it himself, but not prohibitory, it relates to the second clause (in the *Mishnah*): "A woman may be betrothed through herself or through her agent." Is it necessary to state through herself? Said Rabbi Joseph, it is more meritorious through herself than through her agent . . . but there is no prohibition in her case, in accordance with Resh Lakish, who said: It is better for a woman to dwell with a load of grief than to dwell in widowhood.[15]

This is an example of an explanatory *sugyah*. The *sugyah* is analyzing the words of the *Mishnah*. It is assumed that each word in the *Mishnah* is necessary and that nothing is superfluous. In this particular *sugyah*, two seemingly contradictory *memrot* are cited, only to be reconciled later. Thus, the *sugyah* has sought to clarify the text of the *Mishnah*.

Mishnah exegesis, as contained in the amoraic *sugyah*, involves a number of points. Aside from the textual questions, such as the clarification of the names of the sages and the order and exact spelling and meaning of words, the *sugyah* attempts to clarify the textual sources and the precise situation to which the *Mishnah* refers. By uncovering the basic principles underlying the *halakhah* and explaining any contradictions between the *Mishnah* and other source material, a wider dimension of the *halakhah* emerges.

TALMUDIC METHODOLOGY

Instead of using abstract concepts, the Talmud utilizes models. For example, rather than present the laws and principles of damages in abstract terms, the *Mishnah* states:

> The four primary categories of damage (listed in the Torah) are those that derive from the ox, the pit, the *maveh* (the tooth or man) and fire.[16]

Adin Steinsaltz makes the following observation:

> . . . the models cited in the laws of damages, such as horn or foot . . . serve neither as examples nor as parables but operate like modern mathematical or scientific models. The model is utilized in accordance with a series of clearly defined steps, approved by tradition. *Kal va-homer,* for example, is a method applied to a certain model in order to adapt it to another model. Thus there is a high degree of mechanical thought, and no attempt is made to clarify practical or logical problems per se; they are seen rather as complete entities, and their conclusions are of practical or logical significance, though it is not always possible to understand the convoluted methods of the operation itself.[17]

This aversion for the abstract, according to Steinsaltz, is rooted in the relative weakness of all abstract thought. This weakness "lies in the fact that it is constantly creating new terms and concepts, and since they cannot be defined except by use of similarly abstract terms, we can never know whether they constitute a departure from the subject or are still relevant."[18] The talmudic reliance on models in place of abstraction "enables us to draw inferences or examine whether we have diverged from the fundamental issue through abstract thinking on unclear issues."[19]

Another feature of talmudic thought is the tendency to adapt methods and opinions to one another. Though the talmudic text seems to abound with debate, there is an effort to avoid controversy by reducing to a minimum differences of method and opinion.

Sugyah discussions took place at the various academies: in Palestine at Tiberias, Sepphoris, and Lydda; and in Babylonia at Sura and Pumbedita. Discussion and debate was free and open. The *rosh yeshivah* (head of the academy) delivered the lecture. Scholars from the audience would bombard him with questions, which often resulted in a large-scale debate. These and other discussions were eventually to find their way into the Talmud in summary form. Actually, the Talmud is a kind of record of the discussions that took place at the academies.

THE REDACTION OF THE TALMUD

A most perplexing question is how and when the Babylonian Talmud was redacted. In an obscure statement found in the *Gemara,* one learns that the *horaah* (instruction) ended with Ravina and Rav Ashi.[20] Some historians of the Talmud take this statement as an indication that during the fifth century, the Babylonian Talmud underwent a final editing. It was Rav Ashi, who lived from 352 to 427, who devoted the last thirty years of his life to the task of organizing, arranging, and editing the teachings of the *amoraim.* After Rav Ashi's death, Ravina continued his colleague's work and completed the redaction process, bringing the Babylonian Talmud to a close in the year 499.[21]

Other scholars maintain that the final editing of the Babylonian Talmud did not take place at the time of Ravina and Rav Ashi. The reference to Ravina and Rav Ashi at the end of *horaah,* they maintain, relates to the official end of only a certain phase in the history of amoraic teaching. Beginning in the year 455 C.E., the Babylonian Jewish community was severely persecuted. Among other things, this caused a break in the continuous development of the Talmud. The Talmud developed layer by layer, with each subsequent generation of *amoraim* adding to the teachings of the earlier generations. But, unlike previous generations, the scholars and sages who lived toward the end of the fifth century encountered problems in understanding the enormous amount of material that had been accumulated. Most of their efforts, therefore, were devoted to the consolidation of the material they inherited. Thus, the pre-Ravina and Rav Ashi period was looked upon as being more authoritative.[22]

Nevertheless, the Babylonian Talmud remained without a final redaction even after the official end of the amoraic period. The final editorial touches to the Talmud came during the postamoraic, or saboraic age, which lasted about two hundred years. The precise contribution of the *saboraim* has not yet been fully documented. According to Rabbi Sherira Gaon, the eleventh-century *rosh yeshivah* and historian, the *saboraim* explained obscure statements, rendered decisions on undecided cases, and composed various *sugyot*.[23]

THE JERUSALEM TALMUD

What has been said concerning the nature and development of the Babylonian Talmud applies equally to the Jerusalem Talmud. Actually, the name *Jerusalem Talmud* is a misnomer. After the destruction of the Temple in the year 70 C.E. there were no schools of Jewish learning left in Jerusalem. The great *yeshivot* had relocated to the Galilee. A more correct title would be the Talmud of *Eretz Yisrael* (the Talmud of the West).

Nevertheless, in regard to certain aspects, the Palestinian Talmud does differ from its Babylonian counterpart. First, although both Talmuds are written in Aramaic, the Palestinian Talmud is in a western Aramaic dialect, whereas the Babylonian Talmud uses an eastern dialect. Due to geographical differences, the Palestinian Talmud contains many Greek words, whereas the Babylonian has many Persian words.

Of more importance are the differences in style. The Palestinian Talmud is more concise and less dialectical than the Babylonian Talmud. According to Louis Ginzberg, because the Palestinian Talmud was intended for teachers and judges rather than for students of the academies, it was written in a more concise style.[24] However, during amoraic times (third and fourth centuries C.E.), the Jewish community in *Eretz Yisrael* endured great hardships and persecutions. In the year 351, for example, Ursicinus, the Roman commander, repeatedly attacked Tiberias, Sepphoris, and Lydda, the main centers of talmudic learning.[25] Under these conditions it became virtually impossible for the sages to hold extended discourses. For this reason, too, the Palestinian Talmud, unlike the Babylonian Talmud, lacked a period of literary enrichment. It has by and large remained unedited.

Adin Steinsaltz states that the Jerusalem Talmud has come to be regarded "as a kind of index, a stepbrother to the Babylonian Talmud."[26] In many respects, the halakhic views and traditions contained in the Palestinian Talmud are not as authoritative as those of the Babylonian Talmud. Whenever the Jerusalem Talmud contradicts the Babylonian Talmud, the law follows the latter. Only where there is no contradiction, or where the Babylonian Talmud is either silent or unclear, does the authority of the Palestinian Talmud prevail.[27]

No doubt the supremacy of the Babylonian Talmud over the Palestinian is also due to the superior quality of its text, which was redacted with great restraint and precision. Furthermore, inasmuch as the Babylonian *amoraim* already had the Palestinian Talmud available to them (it had been completed about the year 400), their deviant ruling on any matter indicates that they rejected that Talmud's view as unreliable.[28]

Although the two Talmuds come from different locations, neither one is exclusively Babylonian or Palestinian. Each contains *sugyot* originating from its rival community. In fact, there existed a "cross-fertilization" of the academies of Babylonia and Palestine. Rabbis and students traveling between *Eretz Yisrael* and Babylonia brought with them the teachings of *Eretz Yisrael* and, upon return, transmitted the Babylonian teachings to the land of Israel. These emissaries were called *nehutei* ("those who go down"). For when one leaves the land of Israel, it is held that he "goes down." Several of the *nehutei* were merchants, but most were emissaries of the Palestinian academies sent abroad to raise funds for their institutions. The importance of this cross-fertilization should not be minimized, for in this way, the Oral Law was prevented from growing apart in the two main centers. It also helped to create a strong bond between the land of Israel and the Diaspora that continues to this day.

THE "MISSING" TRACTATES

The sixty tractates of the *Mishnah* were studied by the Palestinian and Babylonian *amoraim*. However, there are a number of *Mishnah* tractates, both in the Palestinian and Babylonian Talmuds, for which there is no *Gemara*. The mystery surrounding these so-called missing tractates is most intriguing. Did they exist at one time, only later to disappear, or did they in fact not exist from the start? Scholars have struggled with this problem and have offered different theories.[29] In fact, attempts have been made to reconstruct the missing *Gemara* by extracting material from other sections of the Talmud, thereby creating a so-called synthetic Talmud.

The consensus among scholars is that where complete or near-complete orders of the *Mishnah* lack *Gemara,* such as the orders of *Zeraim* (Seeds) and *Tohorot* (Purities) in the Babylonian Talmud and *Kodashim* (Holy Things) in the Jerusalem Talmud, it most probably never existed. On the other hand, where single tractates or individual chapters are missing *Gemara,* it is very likely that they once did exist, only to be lost in the course of time.[30]

With the completion of the Babylonian Talmud, its text became the primary source of Jewish law. Study of the Talmud continued well into the Middle Ages, with centers in Africa, Asia, and Europe.

THE PUBLICATION AND PRINTING OF THE TALMUD

Soon after the redaction of the Talmud, the need for copies arose. To copy the complete Talmud by hand was no easy task—the Talmud contains approximately two-and-a-half million words. In the period immediately following the final redaction of the Babylonian Talmud, the *geonim* (the heads of the Babylonian academies) were frequently asked to supply copies of the Talmud. Throughout the Middle Ages, copies of the Talmud were therefore at a premium. However, copies became more readily available with the advent of printing. The first known printed edition of the Talmud appeared in Guadalajara, Spain, in 1482—ten years before Columbus discovered America. Other early editions were printed in the Italian towns of Soncino and Pisarro. A major breakthrough in the annals of the printing of the Talmud took place in 1520. At the presses of Daniel Bomberg, a Venetian Christian printer, the first complete edition of the Talmud was printed. Almost all subsequent editions follow the Bomberg format.[31]

5

THE *AGGADAH*

It has been said that the *aggadah* and *halakhah* form the "interwoven strands from which the Talmud was constructed."[1] In fact, about a quarter of the text of the Babylonian Talmud is aggadic. Due to the multifaceted nature of the *aggadah* and its unique literary style, a satisfactory definition of *aggadah* is hard to come by. Scholars tend to define *aggadah* as all the material contained in the Talmud that is not halakhic.[2] Included in *aggadah* are midrashic interpretations of nonlegal character; ethical and homiletical discourses; anecdotes about great personalities, including both biblical personages and talmudic sages; popular legends and folk sayings; theological and philosophical discussions; history; commercial advice; and medical prescriptions.

Though many of the aggadic formulations are not couched in philosophical or theological terminology, and at times seem to lack any systematic structure, these texts, nevertheless, possess great profundity. Maimonides, the great twelfth-century philosopher and talmudist, notes that the *aggadah* is the "essence of truth" in which particles of the divine concepts and fundamental realities are to be found.[3]

AGGADAH COMPARED WITH HALAKHAH

Many of the *aggadot,* both in the Talmud and independent midrashic works, were originally delivered as homiletical discourses at synagogue services. These sermons were usually preached on Sabbath afternoons, with the weekly Torah reading as the main point of departure. Certain sages specialized in the *aggadah* and were known as *Rabbanan de-Aggadata—* sages of the *aggadah.* However, most of the great sages and teachers excelled in both *halakhah* and *aggadah.* Since *aggadah* is easily understood, it was more popular among the people.

The Talmud relates how Rabbi Abbahu and Rabbi Hiyya ben Abba came to a certain place. Rabbi Abbahu expounded *aggadah* and Rabbi Hiyya expounded *halakhah.* All the people left Rabbi Hiyya and went to hear Rabbi Abbahu. This irritated and upset Rabbi Hiyya. Thereupon, Rabbi Abbahu said to him, "I will give you a parable. To what is the matter similar? To two men, one of whom was selling precious stones and the other various kinds of small ware. To whom will the people hurry? Is it not to the seller of various kinds of small ware?"[4] *Halakhah* is compared with precious stones, which not everyone is able to buy and appreciate. *Aggadah* is likened to various kinds of small ware, things that are easy to understand and within everyone's means.

Despite their differences, *halakhah* and *aggadah* coexist. In the Talmud, on the very same page, *halakhah* and *aggadah* are found side by side. A deep, complex legal discussion often gives way to a soaring aggadic discourse. Some of the greatest legal minds were equally at home in the sphere of the *aggadah*. Nevertheless, there is a definite tendency to pit one against the other.

The tension between *halakhah* and *aggadah* has been described by Abraham Joshua Heschel as being between regularity, or the fixed pattern of the law on the one hand, and spontaneity and inwardness of the person on the other hand. According to Heschel:

> Halacha represents the strength to shape one's life according to a fixed pattern; it is a form-giving force. Agada is the expression of man's ceaseless striving which often defies all limitations. Halacha is the rationalization and schematization of living; it defines, specifies, sets measure and limit, placing life into an exact system. Agada deals with man's ineffable relations to God, to other men, and to the world. Halacha deals with details, with each commandment separately; Agada with the whole of life, with the totality of religious life. Halacha deals with the law, Agada with the meaning of the law. Halacha deals with subjects that can be expressed literally; Agada introduces us to a realm which lies beyond the range of expression. Halacha teaches us how to perform common acts; Agada tells us how to participate in the eternal drama. Halacha gives us knowledge; Agada gives us aspiration.[5]

Heschel's characterization of the *halakhah* is somewhat exaggerated and one-sided, yet his point is well taken. The essence of Judaism is a blend of *halakhah* and *aggadah*. To reduce Judaism to either *halakhah* or *aggadah* is to destroy its spirit and essence. Heschel eloquently stated:

> The interrelationship of Halacha and Agada is the very heart of Judaism. Halacha without Agada is dead, Agada without Halakha is wild. . . . Halacha and Agada are correlated: Halakha is the string, Agada is the bow. When the string is tight the bow will evoke the melody. But the string may jar in the fumbler's hand.[6]

EXEGETICAL *AGGADAH*

One of the more frequent types of *aggadah* is exegetical *aggadah*, consisting of homiletical explanations of biblical passages. This form of *aggadah* is also referred to as *midrash* (a searching out of the text). Almost every verse in the Torah is multidimensional. Aside from the *peshat* (the simple meaning of the text), there is the *derash* (homiletical interpretation). In commenting on the biblical verse "and like a hammer that breaks the rock in pieces,"[7] the sages of the Talmud note that "just as the rock is split into many splinters, so also may one biblical verse convey many teachings."[8] The sacred text of the Bible, in the view of the *midrash,* was a "golden nail upon which the *Haggadah* hung its gorgeous tapestries."[9] Each word, each letter, an extra phrase, or a missing detail is intended to teach and enlighten.

To further clarify the mechanics of exegetical *aggadah,* let us turn to the Talmud itself. The *Mishnah* reads as follows:

> A man must not go out with a sword, bow, shield, lance or spear (on the Sabbath); and if he does go out, he incurs a sin-offering. Rabbi Eliezer said: They are ornaments for him. But the Sages maintain, they are merely shameful, for it is said: "And they shall beat their swords into plowshares, and their spears into pruning-hooks, nation shall not lift up sword against nation, neither shall they learn war any more."[10]

This *Mishnah* is concerned with the prohibition against carrying objects on the Sabbath. The issue is whether a man, not under military orders, may go into a public area on the Sabbath carrying a weapon on his person. Rabbi Eliezer sees those objects as nonprohibited ornaments to the man's dress. Thus, he is permitted to go out with them on the Sabbath. The sages, however, view the wearing of such weapons as shameful and contemptuous because they are contrary to the whole spirit of the Sabbath, a day of rest and peace. Thus it is prohibited to wear them on the Sabbath.

The *Gemara,* in discussing this *Mishnah,* asks, "What is Rabbi Eliezer's reason for maintaining that they are ornaments?" "Because," answers the *Gemara,* "it is written 'gird thy sword upon thy thigh, O mighty one, thy glory and thy majesty.' "[11] Rabbi Eliezer supports his view by quoting the psalmist, who praises and glorifies the warrior-king bedecked with his sword. This is taken as an obvious indication that weapons may indeed be worn as adornments.

Rav Kahana, however, voiced his objection to Mar, son of Rav Huna: "But this refers to the words of the Torah!"[12] The sword is a metaphorical expression for Torah learning. Torah learning is Israel's weapon, but it is not to be taken literally. To this, Mar, the son of Rav Huna, replied, "A verse cannot depart from its plain meaning."[13] The sword in Psalms is a metaphor, or *derash,* for Torah. However, since the *peshat* is never to be supplanted by the *derash,* the sword in this case must be regarded as the weapon it is and not just as an ornament.

PESHAT AND DERASH

This talmudic discussion stresses the relationship between the homiletical interpretation and the actual wording of the text. True, a text is a text and whatever meaning one is able to uncover and reveal by means of *midrash* is part of the "divine plan." As a second-century talmudic sage put it, "Turn the Torah and turn it over again, for everything is in it."[14] Still, the plain meaning is the definitive one, of which sight must be never lost. The twelfth-century biblical exegete, Rabbi Abraham ibn Ezra, wrote, "The plain meaning of a verse is not affected by its midrashic interpretation for there are seventy faces to the Torah."[15]

However, this approach is limited to nonhalakhic texts. In

those cases of biblical law where the adoption of the plain meaning would contradict a rabbinically transmitted *halakhah,* Ibn Ezra explains that "we must rely on the accuracy of what they (the sages) say."[16] However, even in those cases where the *halakhah* follows the *derash* the *peshat* still stands, and greater insight may be gained from it as to the hidden or ethical underpinnings of the law. For example, though "an eye for an eye"[17] is interpreted to mean that full monetary compensation is to be paid for bodily damages,[18] the plain meaning of the verse still stands. The words *an eye for an eye* suggest that an injury inflicted upon another's person is not equivalent to damage inflicted upon one's own property. Monetary indemnity alone does not compensate for bodily injuries. While an offender should receive bodily punishment of the same degree and type as that which he inflicted upon the victim, *halakhah* prescribes that in addition to monetary compensation, the offender ought to be bodily punished by flogging.

In practice, however, due to the principle that a person cannot be punished twice for the same crime, such forms of corporal punishment were not carried out. In fact, the *halakhah* prefers monetary indemnity over bodily punishment, for not only is the injured party recompensed for the loss sustained, but the offender is punished, for he must sustain a loss. On the other hand, corporal punishment alone only affords the victim the satisfaction of seeing the offender suffer—a pleasure coming from revenge and a philosophy totally alien to the spirit of talmudic jurisprudence.[19]

Whatever the case may be, the simple sense of the verse "an eye for an eye" gives us greater insight into the spirit of the law.[20]

MIDRASH AND ALLEGORY

Often, *midrash aggadah* is confused with allegory, which interprets a text according to its underlying or hidden meaning.

Allegory goes back to the Stoics, to whom the violence and sexual escapades of the Homeric legends were distasteful and unseemly. By resorting to allegory, they were able to overcome those episodes yet retain the Homeric text as sacred. Philo, an Alexandrian Jew living around the beginning of the present era, used the allegorical method to overcome troubling texts and thus read Platonism into Scripture. Philonic allegory was adopted by the Alexandrian Christian theologians and eventually made its way to Rome. To the early Christian exegetes, allegory was a convenient way of accepting the sanctity of the Old Testament without being troubled by its content and laws.

Unlike *midrash,* allegory denies the plain meaning of the text. *Peshat* does not exist. The literal meaning is removed, revealing something altogether different. Maimonides emphasizes this point most clearly:

With regard to the Midrashim, people are divided into two classes: A class that imagines that the sages have said these things in order to explain the meaning of the text in question, and a class that holds the Midrashim in slight esteem and holds them up to ridicule, since it is clear and manifest that this is not the meaning of the biblical text in question. . . . Neither of the two groups understands that the Midrashim have the character of poetical conceits whose meaning is not obscure for someone endowed with understanding. . . . Thus, the Sages, may their memory be blessed, say: Bar Qappara teaches—"And thou shalt have a paddle upon *azenekha*—thy weapon." Do not read *azenekha,* but *aznekha*—thy ear. This teaches us that whenever a man hears a reprehensible thing, he should put his finger into his ear. Would that I knew whether in the opinion of these ignoramuses, this Tanna believed that to be the interpretation of this text, that such was the purpose of this commandment, that "paddle" means a finger, and that *azenekha*— (thy weapon) refers to the two ears. I do not think that anyone of sound intellect will be of this opinion. But this is a most witty poetical conceit by means of which he instills a noble moral quality, which is in accordance with the fact that just as it is forbidden to tell them, so it is forbidden to listen to obscene things; and he props it up through a reference to a biblical text, as is done in poetical compositions.[21]

HOMILETICAL *AGGADAH*

In addition to exegetical *aggadah,* other types of *aggadah* include the dogmatical *aggadah,* which treats such topics as providence, creation, and messianic times; historical *aggadah,* regarding national and general history; and the ethical *aggadah,* containing proverbs, fables, and stories that are intended to teach moral responsibilities and ethical duties. In many of the latter type of *aggadah,* lofty concepts are often disguised in the form of riddles, legends, and parables. Included also are unbelievable and exaggerated stories, such as the travel tales of Raba bar bar Hana to far-off exotic lands,[22] the depicting of God and His angels as human figures,[23] the various beast fables, like that of the fox and the fishes,[24] and so on.

In order to experience firsthand the flavor and magic of the *aggadah,* let us take a look at an example of talmudic *aggadah.*

It is told of Nahum of Gamzo, an early second-century talmudic sage, that the designation *Gamzo* (this too) was due to the following story:

Once the Rabbis wished to send a present to the Emperor and they deliberated through whom they should send it. They then said: "Let us send it through Nahum of Gamzo, because he is one to whom miracles always happen." So they sent the present through him. On the way, Nahum stopped at an inn over night. During the night the occupants (of the inn) got up, took out everything that was in the bags and filled the bags with dust. When he arrived at his destination, the bags were untied and it was found that they were filled with dust. The Emperor, insulted, said: "The Jews are mocking me," and gave orders to have Nahum executed. Nahum, however, said: "This too is for the good *(gam zu le-tovah)*." Thereupon the prophet Elijah appeared in the disguise of one of them and said to the Emperor: "This is perhaps some of the dust of Abraham, for when Abraham threw dust against an enemy it turned into swords, and when he threw stubble it turned into arrows. . . ." Now there was a certain province which until now they had been unable to conquer. They tried some of the dust against this province and succeeded in conquering it. Thereupon the Emperor took Nahum into the treasury, filled his bags with precious stones and pearls, and dismissed him with great honors. When on his way back he came again to the same inn, the occupants asked him: "What did you bring with you for the Emperor that they honored you so?" "I brought them what I took from here," replied Nahum. Thereupon the occupants of the inn took some of the same dust and brought it to the Emperor. This time the dust did not turn into swords and arrows. All the inhabitants (of the inn) were then executed.[25]

This little tale stresses the need for positive thinking. Nahum's custom of declaring of every happening, no matter how inauspicious it appeared, that "this too is for the best" points to the need for one to have *bitahon* (trust and complete confidence in the divine hand of Providence). In no small way, Nahum's philosophy of "this too, is for the best" has been instrumental in the survival of the Jewish people throughout the ages during the most perilous times.

APPROACHES TO THE UNDERSTANDING OF *AGGADAH*

Many of the *aggadot* raise serious intellectual problems. Aside from the fact that some *aggadot* seem to depart from human reason and common sense, or lack clarity, they are also on occasion incompatible with the Jewish philosophic conception of God. Marc Saperstein comments:

On the face of it, nothing could be more alien to the nature of
systematic religious philosophy, than the aggadah of the classical
literature. By the tenth century, when a far more logically rigorous and coherent style of exposition had come into vogue, the
aggadah was rapidly becoming a source of confusion, consterna-
tion, and embarrassment for many Jews.[26]

To cope with the difficulties posed by some of these *aggadot,*
different approaches were formulated. A fundamentalist approach claimed that all *aggadot* were to be taken literally. The
aggadot were the divinely inspired word of God, and if God did
not want them to be understood literally, as written, they
would not have been so written.[27]

Others reacted to the problematic *aggadot* by denying their
very authority. Some *aggadot,* they argued, lacked authority
inasmuch as they reflected an individual opinion and did not
mirror authentic tradition. According to this view, aggadic
literature is to be classified as "approximate estimations,"
lacking definitive authority; the acceptance or denial of such
aggadot is purely optional.[28]

A middle-of-the-road type of approach seeks to treat the
aggadah as hyperbole. The text of an aggadah is to be understood figuratively. Take for example the following *aggadah:*
"Seven things were created before the world was created:
Paradise, the Torah, the Just, Israel, the Throne of Glory,
Jerusalem and the Name of the Messiah."[29] This is a problematic *aggadah.* How can we speak of things existing before the
universe was created *ex nihile,* out of nothing?

Reason dictates that such aggadic statements are not to be
taken literally. Judah Halevi, the twelfth-century Spanish
Jewish philosopher and poet, commenting on the *aggadah* just
cited, said:

This is similar to the saying of some philosophers: "The primary
thought includes the final deed." It was the object of Divine

wisdom in the creation of the world to create the Torah, which
was the essence of wisdom, and whose bearers are the just, among
whom stands the Throne of Glory and the truly just, who are the
most select, and the proper place for them was Jerusalem, and only
the best of men—the Messiah, son of David, could be associated
with them, and they all entered Paradise. Figuratively speaking
one must assume that they were created prior to the world.[30]

Halevi is saying that before one constructs a building, one first
plans and plots the eventual purpose that building will serve;
so too, the objects of divine wisdom in the creation of the
world preceded its actual creation. It is in this sense that those
seven things mentioned by the Talmud were created before
the actual world was brought into being.

As to why the *aggadot* don't say what they really mean,
Maimonides notes that by disguising the real meaning of such
aggadot the sages, on the one hand, stimulate the interest of
their students, thereby sharpening their wits; on the other
hand, they make it possible that all levels of human understanding benefit from it.[31] Undoubtedly, many attending aggadic discourses did not understand everything they heard.
Nevertheless, they were able to enjoy the homiletics on their
own level.

AGGADIC COLLECTIONS

Aside from the many aggadic sections contained in both the
Babylonian and Palestinian Talmuds, there are numerous independent aggadic works. These *midrashim* devoted to *aggadah*
are divided into two categories: expositional and homiletical.[32] Expositional *midrashim*, like the *Bereshit Rabbah,* are a
running, verse-by-verse commentary on the Pentateuch. The
homiletical type of *midrashim* are composed in the style of
sermons. Basing his talk on the weekly Torah portion, the

preacher would seek to enlighten his audience. Examples of the sermonic type of *midrashim* are the *Midrash Tanhuma* and *Pesikta de-Rav Kahana*.

It is especially interesting to note that no independent midrashic compilations of Babylonian origin have come down to us. The various aggadic collections in our possession came from third- and fourth-century Palestine. It is possible that the Palestinian community, living under the pressure of Roman rule, needed the encouragement and comfort that could be derived from the *aggadah*. In addition, during the third and fourth centuries, Christianity was already firmly established in Palestine. To thwart the spread of Christianity and insulate the Palestinian community against Christian influence, the medium of the *aggadah,* with its inspirational elements, was employed to reinforce the faith.

6
TALMUDIC JURISPRUDENCE

Moshe Silberg, former deputy president of Israel's supreme court, characterized Jewish law in the following manner:

> Jewish law, unlike practically all other legal systems, does not limit itself to the sphere of "between man and man." It also places the relations between man and God in juridical categories; it speaks of them in juridical terms, and it approaches them with a juridical concept. The Holy One, praised be He, in all His glory, is deemed as a kind of legal person, enjoying rights, being subject to obligations, heeding His own precepts, and entering as a subject of civil jurisdiction, as it were, in the complex of relations between Himself and His creatures.[1]

CATEGORIES OF JEWISH LAW

The twofold categorization of Jewish law referred to by Justice Silberg—that of laws between *man and man* and that of

69

laws between *man and God*—points to the all-embracing character of Jewish law. To better understand the breadth of Jewish law as formulated and developed in the Talmud, one need only look at the different departments within the scheme of talmudic jurisprudence.

There are basically three divisions in talmudic law. They are: *Mammanot* (laws of civil and monetary character, such as commercial transactions, loans, and property damages); *Issurai* (concerning issues of ritual or ceremonial law, usually of a religious nature, such as the observance of the Sabbath and Jewish festivals, laws pertaining to prayer and diet, and so forth); and finally, *Nefashot* (cases of capital criminal law, such as manslaughter and homicide). Included in the latter realm are offenses of a purely religious nature, such as idolatry that are subject to the death penalty.

In talmudic law there is no clear distinction between offenses committed by man against man and religious transgressions between man and God. Adin Steinsaltz states, "All the spheres of legal activity are seen only as different aspects of one comprehensive body of teaching."[2] Nevertheless, certain legal rules applicable to civil law may not be applied to those of ritual law. Ritual law, says the Talmud, "cannot be deduced from civil law,"[3] and consequently the principle that a doubtful thing is presumed to have the legal status of the majority of its class applies only to questions of ritual law, not civil matters.[4] The reason for this and other such rulings is that civil law is based upon mutual agreement and contract between the parties and thus subject to waiver *(mehilah)*[5] or presumptive title *(hazakah)*,[6] thereby superseding the majority principle. Likewise, in civil matters the courts are empowered to declare one's property ownerless *(hefker)*.[7]

However, in spite of these and other differences, Jewish law is monistic in the sense that the same concepts, dialectics, and precedents are applicable to all areas of the *halakhah*. In talmudic jurisprudence, civil and religious laws are of the same fabric, and such examples as we have mentioned are the exceptions rather than the rule. To further clarify this idea, there is the basis for the law of "agency" in talmudic jurisprudence.

According to the Talmud, "a man's agent is like himself."[8] Thus, one who acts through an agent is deemed to have performed the act himself. The application of this principle is not restricted to any one category of the *halakhah,* but it is universally applied. Consequently, one may purchase property through an agent; betroth or divorce a spouse by proxy; fulfill a ritualistic religious duty, such as circumcising one's son, through the designation of an agent. In fact, two of the very sources for the rule of agency deal with ritual and not civil ordinances.

Thus, in one instance the Talmud states that the seemingly superfluous word *also* in the verse "Thus you shall also set apart a heave offering unto the Eternal . . ."[9] suggests that one may fulfill his religious obligation of setting aside a heave offering for the priest by proxy. Otherwise it could have simply stated, "You shall set apart a heave offering." The superfluous "also" is taken as an extension of "you"—that the offering may be set aside "also" by whoever is "you"—one who represents you and your intentions, i.e., a proxy.[10]

Likewise, as a source for the laws of agency, the Talmud refers to the biblical passage, "And the whole congregation of Israel shall slaughter it (the paschal lamb)."[11] According to Rabbi Yehoshua ben Korhah, although only one person does the actual slaughtering, the Torah regards it as the act of the entire congregation.[12]

Further proof of the unity and common ground between civil and religious law is seen in the talmudic treatment of sacrifices and temple management. Discussions concerning the consecration and embezzlement *(meilah)* of temple funds and similar matters abound in concepts of a civil nature.

DUTY VERSUS RIGHT

Another unique feature of talmudic jurisprudence is that unlike other legal systems, Jewish law is "duty oriented" rather than "right oriented." In most, if not all, modern systems of law, the concept of *inalienable rights* is at the core of all social laws. Thus, "A" is duty bound not to assault "B" only because "B" has the basic right of being secure in his person against attack.

In talmudic law, the concept of duty rather than right is primary. Failure to come to the assistance of one in distress, in modern jurisprudence, is not deemed a civil wrong or crime, for one does not necessarily have the legal right to demand help from his fellowman. In Jewish law, as formulated in the Talmud, an individual is duty-bound to save his fellowman's life, irrespective of any legal rights on the part of the victim.[13] An interesting application of the duty-oriented scheme is the case of the repayment of a debt. According to Rav Papa, a fourth-century Babylonian teacher, the repayment of a debt has an independent virtuous character—a *mitzvah* (religious moral obligation)—despite the lender's obvious legal right to his money.[14] Following this view, the obligation to repay a loan does not stem from the creditor's right to his money, but rather because of a duty imposed upon the debtor that is independent of any rights. Moshe Silberg aptly states, "The court . . . is not primarily concerned with the indebtedness of the claimant, but with the obligation of the debtor, with his religio-moral obligation, with the performance of his commandment, and it is only as though in a side effect, as a secondary result of the process, does the claimant receive his money."[15] Likewise, Rav Papa would insist that the estate of minor orphans cannot be attached in order to pay their father's debt, inasmuch as minors are exempt from the duty of carrying out *mitzvot*.[16]

The halakhic emphasis on duty rather than right is rooted in the fact that talmudic law is theocentric. Man is expected to act in a specified way because he is enjoined to do so by divine command. Such a system and philosophy of law tends to create a social order in which individuals are aware of their obligations to others. One can only wonder whether today's social disorder is not, in fact, rooted in that emphasis on right over duty, which in no small way contributes to a society in which people are self-centered.[17]

THEOCENTRICITY OF JEWISH LAW

Jewish law is a religious law. It is the word of God *(Torah Min ha-Shamayim)* as revealed to man that constitutes the basis of Jewish law. However, once revealed, it becomes the possession of man, who alone determines the direction of the law based on his understanding of the principles of *halakhah.* Such a theocentric system of law is indeed quite daring. There is a remarkable passage in the Talmud regarding this very theme:

> On a certain occasion Rabbi Eliezer used all possible arguments to substantiate his opinion, but the Rabbis did not accept it. He said, "If I am right, let this carob tree prove it!" Thereupon the carob tree was torn a hundred cubits out of its place. They said, "From a carob tree no proof can be brought." Then he said, "May the canal prove it." The water of the canal flowed backwards. They said, "A canal of water cannot prove anything." Then he said, "May the walls of this house of study prove it." Then the walls of the house bent inwards, as if they were about to fall. Rabbi Joshua rebuked the walls, and said to them, "If the learned dispute about the *halakhah,* what has that to do with you?". . . Then Rabbi Eliezer said: "If I am right, let the Heavens prove it." Then a Heavenly voice said, "what have you against Rabbi Eliezer? The *halakhah* is always with him." Then Rabbi Joshua got up and said, "it is not in Heaven." What did he mean by this? Rabbi Jeremiah

said, the law was given to us from Sinai. We pay no attention to a Heavenly voice. For already from Sinai the law said, "By a majority you are to decide." Rabbi Nathan met Elijah (the prophet) and asked him what God did in that hour. Elijah replied: "He laughed and said, my children have conquered Me."[18]

THE DECISION-MAKING PROCESS

This fascinating episode contains two very important points. First, it stresses the human element in the administration of the *halakhah*. The Torah is *from* heaven but not *in* heaven. Once revealed to man, not even a heavenly voice or a prophetic sign is of any consequence. But does not this human element in the decision-making process tend to secularize religious law? The rabbis of the Talmud were cautious in this respect and emphasized that halakhic, juridical, and legislative powers be entrusted only to those scholars and judges who submit to the yoke of heaven. Scholarship alone is insufficient; a blend of erudition and pious awe are required.

The second point of the episode concerns the idea of the absolute rule of law. Even the lawgiver is bound by the law he has given and must submit to the accepted interpretation of the authorized interpreters. The law concerning doubtful cases is that "by a majority you are to decide,"[19] and even though for the lawgiver himself there is no doubtful case, still he must accept the judgment as pronounced by the empowered court. God Himself declared, "My children have conquered Me."[20]

Although this notion of absolute law is commonplace, in ancient times it was not the case. Dio Cassius, the second-century Roman historian, relates how the Roman senate accorded Augustus (24 B.C.E.) the right of supremacy over both himself and the laws, so that he might obey only those laws he chose to obey and disregard the others.[21] Contrasting the

Jewish attitude of absolute law to the Roman law of his day, Rabbi Elazar states:

> On the king the law is not binding. Ordinarily when an earthly king issues a decree, if he wishes he can keep it, if he wishes—only others must keep it; but the Holy One, praised be He, is not so. When He issues a decree, He is the first to heed it. Why is this so? It is written: "And they shall keep my charge . . . I am the Lord"— I am He who was first to keep the commandments of the Torah.[22]

THE DEATH PENALTY

Then there is the area of capital offenses and the death penalty. There are, according to the Bible, thirty-six crimes punishable by death. These offenses range from murder and adultery to desecration of the Sabbath and idolatry. The fact that some crimes are punishable by death and others are not is due to the severity of the particular crime. What determines the severity of a crime is the particular purpose of the law. The more fundamental and basic the purpose of a particular law, the more serious is the crime when that law is violated. Thus, murder is punishable by death because it is essentially a desecration of God's image, for "He did create man in the image of God."[23] Likewise, desecration of the Sabbath is a capital crime because it undermines the belief in God as the Creator of the world.

The laws concerning capital punishment are detailed in the *Mishnah* and *Gemara* of *Makkot* and *Sanhedrin*. Some of the outstanding features of talmudic criminal law are the following: There is no jury. Cases of capital offenses are tried before a court of twenty-three judges. There are no defense or prosecuting attorneys; the members of the court are expected to argue in the defense. It is essential in all capital cases that there be at least two trustworthy witnesses. The witnesses, in addition to establishing the validity of the accusation, also perform the role of prosecutor. Only eyewitness testimony is acceptable. Circumstantial evidence is not admissible. The witnesses are interrogated concerning the exact time, place, and persons involved in the crime. Any material discrepancy discovered in the testimony of the witnesses results in immediate acquittal of the accused. Of utmost importance is the requirement that the witnesses had warned the accused that he was about to commit a crime punishable by death. This requirement is called *hatraah* (sounding the alarm). Finally, the accused is presumed innocent until proven guilty.[24]

In recent times there has been some discussion concerning the Jewish position on the death penalty. Though capital punishment is sanctioned by the Bible, the position of the sages of the Talmud is not all that clear. Discussion centers around the following *Mishnah:*

> Rabbi Tarfon and Rabbi Akiva say: Were we in the Sanhedrin (the highest Jewish court) no man would ever have been put to death. Rabban Simon ben Gamliel says: They too, would multiply spillers of blood in Israel.[25]

The Talmud, in discussing Rabbi Tarfon and Rabbi Akiva's view, inquires as to how they would carry out their policy. It is suggested that the witnesses would be examined with intimate questions, such as, "Did you take note whether the victim was suffering from some fatal affliction or was he perfectly healthy?" And should their reply be "perfectly healthy" they might be asked, "Maybe the sword only severed an internal lesion?" By employing such detailed and intimate questions, an "interrogation of the unknowable," the witnesses would be in no position to urge the death penalty on grounds of human weakness because man is unable to know every iota of fact.[26] Whether, as Gerald Blidstein writes, "the source of their opposition was not a fear of killing the innocent but a reluctance to kill the guilty,"[27] the goal of Rabbis Akiva and Tarfon was to eliminate the death penalty.

Rabban Simon ben Gamliel, on the other hand, maintained that the death penalty is needed. Capital punishment, according to his view, is both useful and moral—useful, for it serves as a deterrent; moral, because it is a divine ordinance.

Of course, there is a metaphysical aspect to the death penalty. When one violates God's law he deserves to be condemned. The commission of a capital offense—a crime of the highest order—is punishable by death. The death penalty is an expression of God's absolute condemnation of man. The value of human life is derived from God's law, and such violations of His moral code destroy the very worth of human life.[28]

The final ruling follows the view of Rabban Simon ben Gamliel. However, the death penalty was rarely carried out due to the technicalities and weightiness of the law.

The scope of talmudic law is quite broad. It includes all areas of life, both religious and social. So long as the Jews lived in their own homeland, the implementation of a talmudic system of jurisprudence was possible. However, what place and role could Jewish law have had in the Diaspora, where Jews were expected to abide by the secular laws of their adopted nation?

"THE LAW OF THE KINGDOM IS THE LAW"

The third-century Babylonian teacher, Samuel, coined the expression *Dina de—Malkhuta Dina* (the Law of the Kingdom is the Law).[29] According to this principle, the non-Jewish legal system functions as an extension of Jewish law. Leo Landman maintains that the principle of *Dina de-Malkhuta Dina* is based upon Samuel's knowledge and understanding of the difficulties encountered in the Diaspora. Jewish law and the law of the kingdom wherever Jews lived could differ and be antagonistic to each other. Hence, in formulating this concept, Samuel provided Jews of all ages and countries with a modus vivendi.[30]

Essentially, the principle of *Dina de-Malkhuta Dina* says that when Jewish laws of *Mammanot* (civil, monetary, and real estate) come into conflict with the secular law, they may be set aside in favor of the latter. Samuel's doctrine in no way applies to ritual law, such as Sabbath observance, marriage and divorce, and the dietary laws.[31] Needless to say, even in respect to civil matters, laws of the state or kingdom that are unfair, discriminatory, or unjust do not fall into the category of *Dina de-Malkhuta Dina.*

Some medieval talmudic commentators viewed Samuel's dictum as a pact or agreement between the king and his subjects. One source, in fact, describes *Dina de-Malkhuta Dina* as a feudal arrangement, whereby obedience to the monarch's laws is expected in return for his granting permission to the Jews to settle in his land.[32]

With the establishment of the modern state of Israel in 1948, the question concerning the application of *Dina de-Malkhuta Dina* to legislation enacted by the Kenneset was raised. Basically, the issue was whether Samuel's doctrine is limited only to non-Jewish kings and governments, or whether it also applies to the laws and statutes of Jewish kings and Jewish governments.

To resolve this problem, it is necessary to understand how *Dina de-Malkhuta Dina* operates. Actually, it is divided into two functional areas. First, there are the biblical rights granted to all kings, which enable them to establish and conduct their kingdoms. Second, *Dina de-Malkhuta Dina* involves the necessity to establish an equitable and just legal system.[33] The first area, that of the rights granted to states and governments to establish and conduct their affairs, applies to Jewish as well as non-Jewish sovereigns and governments. However, with re-

gard to the valid establishment of legal systems, this area of
Dina de-Malkhuta Dina applies only to non-Jewish governments. A Jewish king or a Jewish government in Israel, most
authorities agree, should adopt and follow the legal system of
the Torah, including its civil aspects.

In line with this approach, the decisions of the Israeli government concerning issues of security, military draft, and
matters of taxation are validated by *Dina de-Malkhuta Dina*.
However, in cases of monetary or civil questions, the Jewish
government is expected to follow the halakhic legal system.[34]

7

THE TALMUDIC SAGE

The sages or *(Hakhamim)* molded the life of the Jewish people and greatly influenced their understanding of their past, present, and future. Actually, the institution of the sages predates the talmudic period. Indeed, the *Zekanim* (elders of the biblical period), and the prophets of ancient times are the forerunners of the *Hakhamim* of talmudic times. Historically speaking, the period of the sages encompasses the Men of the Great Assembly (founded by Ezra after the Restoration), the *sofrim*, the *tannaim*, and the *amoraim*, the expounders of the *Mishnah* and creators of the *Gemara*.

One of the earliest descriptions of the sages is found in the apocryphal book of Ben Sira. Writing between the years 190 and 170 B.C.E., Ben Sira describes the sages as follows:

> Learning is the privilege of leisure. Husbandmen and artisans are the support of the social structure, but wholly occupied as they must be in their several callings and often highly expert in them, they have no time for the wide-ranging studies that make the

scholar. . . . Different is the case of the man who gives his whole
mind to it, and concentrates his thought on the law of the Most
High. He will seek out the wisdom of all the ancients, and occupy
himself with the study of prophecies, and pay attention to expositions of famous men, and will penetrate into the elusive turns of
parables. He will search out the hidden meaning of proverbs, and
will be versed in the enigmas of parables. He will serve among the
magnates and appear in the presence of the ruler. He will travel in
foreign countries, for he has experience of good and evil among
men. He will resolve to rise early to the service of the Lord his
Creator, and will make his petition to the Most High; he will open
his mouth in prayer, and beseech forgiveness for his sins. . . . He
will make public the instruction he has to impart, and his pride
will be in (knowledge of) the Law of the Covenant of the Lord.[1]

Ben Sira's sage is thus not only a jurist but a scholar and
teacher as well, a pious man whose dedication to both Torah
and God is of the highest order. Unlike the ivory-towered
scholar, the sage will serve among the magnates, travel abroad,
and above all "make public the instruction he has to impart."[2]

The dominant role played by the sages in Jewish life began
at the time of the Restoration, in 444 B.C.E., during the days of
Ezra and the Men of the Great Assembly. It gained further
impetus in the time of Rabbi Yohanan ben Zakkai and the
establishment of the Sanhedrin at Yavne, following the destruction of the Second Temple in the year 70 C.E.

JUDGES AND SCHOLARS

The sages were primarily engaged in judging, in scholarship,
and in religious-communal leadership. As judges, the sages
were called upon to render legal decisions in the realms of
religious, civil, and criminal law. Besides being expertly

trained in all facets of the law, members of the judiciary were also expected to demonstrate excellence in moral and character development. Judges had to show patience, humility, and respect. The extent of authority and law enforcement wielded by the rabbinic courts varied from period to period, especially since the authority of the courts was restricted and hampered in those times when Jewish autonomy was severely curtailed.

Of primary importance was the role of the scholar. To qualify as a scholar *(talmid hakham)* one had to be capable of studying and understanding the Torah. However, intellectual ability was not enough. Academic excellence had to be accompanied by noble human behavior. A scholar who did not practice what he preached was not deemed a scholar. "Anyone whose fear of sin precedes his wisdom, his wisdom shall endure. But one whose wisdom precedes the fear of sin, his wisdom shall not endure."[3] So teaches a *Mishnah* text in tractate *Avot.*

THE WELL-ROUNDED TORAH SCHOLAR

The following talmudic teaching stresses the well-rounded personality of the Torah scholar:

> Torah is greater than priesthood or monarchy, since monarchy calls for thirty qualities and priesthood for twenty-four, while Torah demands forty-eight attributes: Audible study, distinct pronunciation, understanding and discernment of the heart, awe, reverence, meekness, cheerfulness, ministering to the Sages, attaching oneself to colleagues, discussion with disciples, sedateness, knowledge of the Bible and of *Mishnah.*

It goes on to list these further attributes of the well-rounded Torah scholar:

Moderation in business, moderation in pleasure, in sleep, in conversation, in laughter. He must also demonstrate good character by forbearance, by a good heart, by faith in the wise, by acceptance of chastisement, by recognizing one's place, by rejoicing in one's portion, by putting a fence to one's words, by claiming no merit for oneself, by being beloved, by loving the Almighty, by loving mankind, by loving justice, rectitude and reproof, by avoiding honor, by not boasting of one's learning, by not delighting in giving decisions, by bearing the yoke with others, by judging one's fellow favorably, by showing him the truth, by leading him to peace, by being composed in one's study, by asking, answering, hearing and adding thereto, by learning with the object of teaching, by learning with the object of practicing, by making one's master wiser, fixing attention upon his discourse, by quoting things in the name of their author.[4]

Indeed, the ideal Torah scholar was the personification of Torah itself.

Most scholars supported themselves by engaging in various professions and trades—we hear of Rabbi Yohanan the shoemaker, Rabbi Yitzhak the blacksmith, and Hillel the woodchopper, among others. However, there were those sages who advocated exclusive devotion to Torah study. The Talmud states:

Our Rabbis taught: "And you shall gather in your corn." What is to be learnt from these words? Since it says, "This Book of the Law shall not depart out of your mouth." I might think that this injunction is to be taken literally. Therefore it says, "And you shall gather in your corn," which implies that you are to combine the study of Torah with a wordly occupation. This is the view of Rabbi Yishmael. Rabbi Shimon bar Yohai says: Is that possible? If a man ploughs in the ploughing season, and sows in the sowing season, and reaps in the reaping season, and threshes in the threshing season, and winnows in the season of wind, what is to become of the Torah? No. But when Israel performs the will of

God, their work is performed by others . . . and when Israel does
not perform the will of God their work is carried out by themselves . . . nor is this all, but the work of others is done by them.[5]

Similarly, dividing one's time properly between learning
Torah and praying is discussed. The question is raised, concerning those pious men of old who used to devote nine hours
a day to prayer, as to whether this left them sufficient time to
study Torah.[6]

Ephraim Urbach points out that such problems as concern
the studying of Torah and pursuing a trade or profession "did
not cease troubling, complicating, and confusing the circle of
the sages."[7]

Not only was the talmudic sage versed in Torah, but he also
possessed great secular and general knowledge. Such pursuits
by the *Hakham* was chiefly to serve the ends of Torah. A
knowledge of both animal and human anatomy, for example,
was essential to understand dietary laws and questions of
family purity; familiarity with astronomy and mathematics
was necessary to grasp the laws pertaining to the calendar.
Concerning the study of languages, a third-century scholar
remarked, "There are four languages one ought to use: Greek
for the art of poetry, Latin for the terms of military command,
Aramaic for elegies and Hebrew for daily speech."[8]

RELIGIOUS-COMMUNAL LEADERSHIP

Although he was not a professional rabbi in the modern sense,
the sage was a religious and communal leader. While tension
sometimes existed between the laity and the sages, they were
treated with respect and dignity as holy men. However, it
appears that in the synagogue the sage had no special role. He
did not preside over the prayer meetings; any Jew was able to

lead the service and read from the Torah. Only on special occasions, such as in times of drought, were the sages called upon to beseech the Almighty.[9]

On matters of *halakhah* the sages were consulted by the people. Yet, the three areas of laws most scrupulously observed by Babylonian Jewry were those of *kashrut* (dietary rules), family purity, and the Sabbath.[10] On matters pertaining to these laws, the sages were frequently consulted by the people. Concerning elements of the supernatural and theological matters, the sage was the authority par excellence. Similarly, he was able to pray effectively due to his knowledge of the proper times and forms of prayer.[11] The sages also lectured the people on Sabbath afternoons about the Law and weekly Torah portion.

Those sages connected with the office of Patriarch and Exilarch, the political heads of Palestine and Babylonian Jewry respectively, tended to the economical, political, and social needs of the community. It is said of Rav Huna, for example, that on every cloudy day he would go out and survey the whole town. He would order every wall that looked unsafe to be torn down. If the owner could rebuild it, he did so, and if not, Rav Huna would rebuild it at his own expense. Whenever he discovered a medicine, he would fill a jug with it and suspend it above the doorstep and announce, "Whoever wants to, let him come and take." When Rav Huna ate bread, he would open his door wide and declare, "Whoever is in need, let him come and eat."[12]

Two Biographical Sketches

The biographical sketches of two leading talmudic teachers give a better understanding of the talmudic sage. Most of the data and source material about these men comes from the

Talmud in the form of stories, legends, and maxims. The legal thinking and juridical decisions of the sages also reveal a great deal about their intellectual prowess and methodology of learning. At the same time, it exposes the inner nature of the man.

HILLEL HA-NASI

Hillel ha-Nasi, who was one of the greatest sages of the Second Temple period, was born in Babylonia. Aside from the fact that his mother hailed from the family of King David[13] and his father from the tribe of Benjamin,[14] nothing more is known of his parents and early childhood. At the age of forty,[15] Hillel came to *Eretz Yisrael* to study at the academy of Shemayah and Avtalion.[16] According to the well-known legend, he earned his living as a woodchopper, paying half of his daily earnings to the gatekeeper of the academy in order to gain entry into the study hall. One day Hillel found no work, and the gatekeeper refused to admit him without payment. Thereupon, Hillel climbed up to the roof of the academy and, sitting on the skylight, listened to the lecture below. Engrossed in the lecture and oblivious of the winter weather, Hillel was soon covered with falling snow. During the class, the instructor noticed a shadowy figure on the roof. Thus the half-frozen Hillel was rescued.[17]

Eventually Hillel was appointed to the office of *nasi* (president of the Sanhedrin). The circumstances surrounding that appointment are as follows: In the year 31 B.C.E., the eve of Passover fell on the Sabbath. Inasmuch as the Passover sacrifice must be slaughtered on the eve of Passover, the Sons of Betayra, who headed the Sanhedrin, had forgotten the *halakhah* as to whether or not the slaughtering of the Paschal lamb overrides the Sabbath. Hillel was summoned and the

problem was submitted to him. Using principles of hermeneutics, Hillel proved that the Passover sacrifice does indeed
take precedence over the Sabbath. However, all his proofs
were refuted by the Sons of Betayra. It was only after Hillel
informed the Sanhedrin that he had received this ruling from
his two great teachers, Shemayah and Avtalion, that it was
unanimously accepted. The members of the Sanhedrin were so
impressed with Hillel's erudition and dedication that they
appointed him *nasi*.[18]

Though elevated to high office and having gained much
fame, Hillel continued to live a humble life. He often said, "If
anyone makes personal use of the crown of Torah learning for
selfish ends, he shall soon be gone."[19] It is related that Hillel
"bought for a certain poor man who was of a good family, a
horse to ride upon and a slave to run before him. On one
occasion he could not find a slave to run before him, so Hillel
himself ran before the man for three miles."[20]

THE GREAT HUMILITY OF HILLEL

Hillel is best known for his great humility and pursuit of
peace. One of his well-known maxims was, "Be of the disciples of Aaron, loving peace, pursuing peace. Be one who loves
his fellow-creatures and draws them near to Torah."[21] Hillel's
love of humanity and pursuit of peace is testified to in this
classic story:

> Two men wagered that whichever one could make Hillel lose his
> temper would win four hundred zuzim from the other. On a
> Friday afternoon, while Hillel was taking a bath (in preparation
> for the Sabbath) one of the men passed by his door and shouted:
> "Where is Hillel? Where is Hillel?" Hillel wrapped in a robe
> emerged and asked the man what he desired. The man said: "I
> have a question to ask you. Why do the Babylonians have round
> heads?" "That is a profound question," Hillel replied. "It is

because their midwives are not trained properly." The man departed, and returned a little while later. Again he shouted—"Where is Hillel? Where is Hillel?" And again the Sage appeared in his robe. The question this time was: "Why do the people of Tadmor (Palmyra) have slanting eyes?" "This too," said Hillel, "is a profound question. It is because they live in a sandy country and the slits prevent sand from penetrating their eyes." Again the man departed, only soon to return. "Why are the feet of the Africans so broad?" asked the man this time. "This too is a profound question," Hillel answered. "It is because they live in a marshy land." Thereupon, the man said that he had many more questions to ask the Sage, but was afraid that the great Sage would get angry with him. Hillel sat down and told the man to ask all his questions. The man then said: "Are you the Hillel whom they call Prince of Israel?" "Yes," replied Hillel. "If so," the man declared angrily, "may there be no more like you in Israel!" "But why, my son?" asked Hillel. "Because on account of you I have lost four hundred zuzim!" replied the man. To this Hillel responded: "It is better for you to lose four hundred zuzim, and even another four hundred, than that Hillel should lose his temper!"[22]

Similarly, the famous stories of Hillel and proselytes demonstrate his extraordinary patience and sympathetic attitude toward those wishing to embrace the Jewish faith. When a certain heathen came to Shammai, Hillel's associate and colleague, he stated: "If you can teach me the whole Torah while I stand on one foot, you can make me a Jew." Shammai pushed him away with the builder's measuring stick that was in his hand. Hillel's response to the heathen was, "What is hateful to you, do not do to your neighbor; that is the whole Torah, the rest is commentary, go study."[23]

HILLEL'S LEGAL PRONOUNCEMENTS

Of Hillel's numerous rulings, perhaps the most famous is that of the *prosbol*. The word *prosbol* is of Greek origin and literally means "before the council." According to the Bible, the sabbatical year required that all debts or loans be remitted or canceled in that year: "At the end of every seven years, you shall celebrate the remission year . . . that every creditor shall remit any debt owed by his neighbor and brother. . . ."[24] However, it was brought to Hillel's attention that people were not lending money to the needy for fear that the loan would be remitted in the sabbatical year.[25] To overcome this problem, Hillel introduced the *prosbol.* This is a document, when drawn up by the creditor, that protects the debt owed to him from being remitted. Upon execution of the *prosbol,* custody of all debts is awarded to the *Bet Din.*[26]

On the surface it appears as if Hillel, resorting to legal fiction, modified or abolished biblical law. However, Hillel did no such thing. The *prosbol* as instituted by Hillel is based on a well-established biblical halakhic principle known as *Hefker Bet Din Hefker* (ownerless by the court is ownerless).[27] This means that a court has the right to confiscate money and property when in its judgment it serves to avert a breakdown of the law. Thus, during the sabbatical year, all debts are in fact remitted. However, in light of the situation that people were not lending money to the needy for fear that the debt would be remitted, the court was empowered to confiscate the amount of the debt and restore it to the lender.[28]

BET HILLEL AND BET SHAMMAI

Both Hillel and Shammai were founders of schools known by their respective names—Bet Hillel and Bet Shammai. The two schools engaged in numerous debates and discussions on Jewish law. Of the 316 controversies between the two schools recorded in the Talmud, the school of Shammai ruled more leniently than the school of Hillel in only fifty-five cases. Bet

Hillel lived up to the pattern and standards set by its founder, who was patient, mild-tempered, and lenient without compromising or deviating from the law. Hillel's personality would serve as a model of conduct for future generations.

RABBI SHIMON BEN LAKISH: A THIRD-CENTURY AMORAIC TEACHER

Turning to the amoraic period, the colorful personality of Rabbi Shimon ben Lakish is most striking. Rabbi Shimon ben Lakish (Resh Lakish),[29] was a third-century Palestinian teacher. Unfortunately, little is known of his childhood years. However, in his youth, due to harsh economic conditions, he sold himself to men who hired participants in gladiatorial contests.[30] He also worked as a plantation guard.[31] It is probably concerning this early period of Resh Lakish's life that the *aggadah* recounts:

> One day Rabbi Yohanan was bathing in the Jordan river when Resh Lakish saw him and leapt into the Jordan after him. Said Rabbi Yohanan to him: "Your strength should be for the Torah." "Your beauty," replied Resh Lakish, "should be for women." "If you will repent," said Rabbi Yohanan, "I will give you my sister in marriage, who is more beautiful than I." Resh Lakish undertook to repent. . . . Subsequently Rabbi Yohanan taught him Bible and Mishnah and made him into a great man.[32]

With great devotion and diligence, Resh Lakish studied Torah and in time became one of the most esteemed scholars in Rabbi Yohanan's academy. In the course of time, Rabbi Yohanan and Resh Lakish became close colleagues. The closeness between the two scholars is dramatically depicted in the following story:

Resh Lakish died, and Rabbi Yohanan was plunged into deep grief. Said the Rabbis, "Who shall go to ease his mind? Let Rabbi Eleazar ben Pedat go, whose disquisitions are very subtle." So he went and sat before him; and on every dictum uttered by Rabbi Yohanan he observed: "There is a *Baraita* which supports you." "Are you as the son of Lakisha?" he complained. "When I stated a law, the son of Lakisha used to raise twenty-four objections, to which I gave twenty-four answers, which consequently led to a fuller comprehension of the law; while you say, 'A *Baraita* has been taught which supports you': do I not know myself that my dicta are right?" Thus he went on rending his garments and weeping, "Where are you, O son of Lakisha, where are you, O son of Lakisha"; and he cried thus until his mind turned. Thereupon, the Rabbis prayed for him, and he died.[33]

Resh Lakish's keenness of mind and analytical ability has been described by one talmudic teacher as that of "uprooting mountains and grinding them against each other."[34] Like the true sage, Resh Lakish did not let his academic studies stand in the way of common decency and human compassion. His love for the Jewish people was as great as his love for Torah. In the *midrash* it is told that Resh Lakish and Rabbi Abbahu once went to the city of Caesarea, a place inhabited by a large number of hellenized Jews who did not keep the precepts of the Torah. Rabbi Abbahu denounced the inhabitants of Caesarea as sinners and blasphemers. Thereupon, Resh Lakish alighted from his donkey, took a fistful of sand, and put it in Rabbi Abbahu's mouth, saying, "God does not want evil spoken of Israel."[35] During the difficult times, when *Eretz Yisrael* was under Roman military rule, it was Resh Lakish who comforted the people with his many homilies.

Small wonder that the sages were held in such reverence by the people, not only in their own time but throughout the ages as well.

8

THE GROWTH AND DEVELOPMENT OF TALMUDIC EXEGESIS

With the end of the amoraic period in the year 500 C.E. and the completion of the Talmud by the year 700, the Talmud emerged as the basic text and final word on Jewish law. As a result, copies of the Talmud were found far and wide in the study houses and private libraries of Jews living in Europe, Asia, and Africa. Still, the mastery of the Talmud text was a difficult matter. First, the Aramaic-Hebrew in which the Talmud was written was not always the language of Jews living outside Babylonia. Second, to those untrained in talmudic dialectics, the structure and basic approach of the *Gemara* often appeared disjointed and baffling.

WRITINGS OF THE *GEONIM*

So long as the Talmud remained without some form of elucidation and commentary, it was virtually a closed book for many people. At first, the *geonim* (the heads of the academies in posttalmudic Babylonia) were the chief expositors of the

Talmud. They were the heirs to the *amoraim*—the expounders of the *Mishnah* and the *saboraim*—the teachers in the first two centuries after the Talmud's compilation. Far-off Jewish settlements would inquire of the *geonim* as to the precise meaning of a talmudic text or the clarification of a difficult term. These early talmudic commentaries of the *geonim* were in the form of letters responding to the requests of different communities.[1] Because they were in response to a specific issue or question, they often lacked an overall completeness or systematic structure. Near the close of the geonic era, during the eleventh century, more complete and systematic talmudic commentaries began to appear in Babylonia.[2] For almost a thousand years, many of these geonic commentaries remained in obscurity. Only recently, since the discovery at the end of the last century of the Cairo *Genizah* (the storeroom for books and documents that were no longer usable), did they begin to come to light again.

New Centers of Jewish Learning

With the decline of Babylonian Jewry in the eleventh century, new centers of Jewish learning developed in Spain, Italy, France, Germany, and North Africa. Gradually, rabbinic authority was transferred from Babylonia to the West. The following medieval legend serves to explain this transference of power:

> The commander of a fleet, whose name was Ibn Rumahis, left Cordova (Spain), having been sent by the Muslim King of Spain, Abd ar-Rahman an-Nasir. This commander of a mighty fleet set out to capture the ships of the Christians and the towns that were close to the coast. They sailed as far as the coast of Palestine and swung about to the Greek Sea and the islands therein. Here (on the Greek Sea) they encountered a ship carrying four great scholars,

who were travelling from the city of Bari to a city called Sefastin, and who were on their way to a Kallah convention. Ibn Rumahis captured the ship and took the sages prisoner. One of them was Rabbi Husiel, the father of Rabbenu Hananel; another was Rabbi Moses, the father of Rabbi Hanok, who was taken prisoner with his wife and son, Rabbi Hanok; the third was Rabbi Shemariah ben Rabbi Elhanan. (The name of the fourth sage is not known.) . . . The sages did not tell a soul about themselves or their wisdom. The commander sold Rabbi Shemariah in Alexandria of Egypt; Rabbi Shemariah proceeded to Fostat where he became head of the academy. Then he sold Rabbi Husiel on the coast of Ifrqiya (Africa). From there the latter proceeded to the city of Qairawan, where he became the head of the academy and where he begot his son Rabbenu Hananel. Then the commander arrived at Cordova where he sold Rabbi Moses along with Rabbi Hanok (Rabbi Moses' wife had drowned at sea). He was redeemed by the people of Cordova, who were under the impression that he was a man of no education. Now there was in Cordova a synagogue that was called the College Synagogue, where a judge by the name of Rabbi Nathan the Pious, who was a man of distinction, used to preside. However, the people of Spain were not thoroughly versed in the words of our rabbis, of blessed memory. Nevertheless, with the little knowledge they did possess, they conducted a school and interpreted the traditions more or less accurately. Once Rabbi Nathan, when lecturing on a particular Talmudic topic, was unable to explain it correctly. Thereupon, Rabbi Moses, who was seated in the corner like an attendant, arose before Rabbi Nathan and objected to his explanation. When Rabbi Nathan and his students heard his words, they marvelled to each other and asked him to explain the law to them. This he did quite properly. Then each of them propounded to him all their difficulties which they had, and he replied to them out of the abundance of his wisdom. . . . Rabbi Nathan deferred his authority to Rabbi Moses, declaring: "I am no longer judge. This man, who is garbed in rags and is a stranger, is my master, and I shall be his disciple from this day on." Rabbi Moses was appointed judge of the community of Cordova. The report of all this spread throughout the Maghreb (Moslem countries west of Egypt) and students came to study under him. Moreover, all questions which had formerly been addressed to the Babylonian academies were now directed to him.[3]

SEPHARDIC AND ASHKENAZIC CENTERS

Though the historical accuracy of this story may be questioned,[4] talmudic learning was no longer the exclusive possession of the Babylonian academies. With the arrival of Rabbi Husiel in Qairawan and Rabbi Moses in Cordova, North Africa and Spain began to emerge as centers of talmudic learning. From the North African school we possess two important works of talmudic commentary: a commentary on the Talmud by Rabbi Hananel and *A Key to the Locks of the Talmud* (Sefer ha-Mafteah) by Rabbi Nissim, which dealt with selected topics. In the course of time, various genres of talmudic commentaries were composed by the Spanish school, such as Maimonides' *Mishnah* commentary and the novellas of Rabbi Moses ben Nahman (Nahmanides, 1194–1270) and Rabbi Shlomo ben Aderet (Rashbah, 1235–1310). Generally speaking, the Spanish school concentrated on the codified law, and consequently many of their commentaries follow a more comprehensive view of matters without excessive preoccupation with detail and particulars.

Unlike the geonic talmudic works and those of the Maghreb are the works that were authored by Ashkenazic, European scholars. Until the ninth century, Ashkenazic talmudic scholarship was centered in southern Italy. Toward the end of this period, a number of Jewish families moved to northern Italy and France. Encouraged by the Carolingian rulers, some of these families migrated farther north and west, settling in the Rhineland.[5] Ashkenazic Jewry, unlike its Sephardic counterpart, was more aligned with Palestine, via Greece and Italy, than with Babylonia. Many Ashkenazic practices, especially in the liturgy, have their origin in Palestinian custom and ritual.[6]

The rabbinic scholarship of the communities of northern Europe was of a high caliber and based on a continuation of family traditions going as far back as the seventh and eighth centuries. Irving A. Agus, a noted historian of the medieval period, writes:

> This scholarship consisted mainly of the following three elements: (a) the text of the Babylonian Talmud; (b) an elaborate commentary on this Talmud, transmitted orally from generation to generation, which contained, in addition to an exact and accurate interpretation of the text, also an explanation of the manner in which each ruling was to be applied to actual situations; and (c) an elaborate system of public law, governing all phases of community organization and administration, transmitted orally through generations, mainly by observing actual practice.[7]

Due to the fact that during this period, in the tenth century, the Jews of northwestern Europe enjoyed self-rule, talmudic law was not merely an academic pursuit but was applied to actual everyday living.

Thus, the early European talmudic commentaries in our possession are essentially part of that orally transmitted commentary as studied in the Franco-German academies. Agus describes the development of these commentaries:

> This oral commentary slowly solidified into a rigid phraseology, so that every teacher used more or less the same phrases in explaining a text of the Talmud. A young student of Lucca, Mainz, or Paris, learned from his teacher to read the text of the Talmud phrase by phrase and to interpolate between each phrase a few exact words—words that had once been carefully and painstakingly chosen, and then traditionally transmitted—that accurately elucidated that phrase in its particular context. At the end of a small portion of the text, a rigidly memorized sentence or

two served as the explanation of that portion. The young students would faithfully repeat the text together with the interpolated oral explanations until the exact wording of the whole was well fixed in memory. Some students wrote down brief portions of these explanations on the margin of their text, while others relied completely on memory. Occasionally a student would add a brief explanation he had heard from his teacher, often appending the latter's name. Thus, there came into being, among Italian, French and German Jews, a commentary on the Talmud that was the result of the teachings of many generations of scholars.[8]

An example of such a commentary to the Talmud is the commentary of Rabbenu Gershom, an eleventh-century teacher at the talmudic academy of Mainz. There he taught the Talmud according to the orally transmitted commentary, interpolating his own ideas and observations. Erroneously, the entire commentary that bears his name was attributed to Rabbenu Gershom. However, he was not the originator of or sole contributor to this work.[9] Commentaries such as the one ascribed to Rabbenu Gershom were to become the source for several written commentaries; the most famous of these was the commentary of Rashi.

RASHI: EXEGETE PAR EXCELLENCE

Rashi, which is the Hebrew acronym for Rabbi Shlomo Yitzhaki, was born in the year 1040 in Troyes, a city in northern France. During his student days at the talmudic academies of Worms and Mainz, Rashi engaged in copious note-taking. He recorded the orally transmitted commentary of Ashkenazic Jewry to the Talmud. Often Rashi was careful to use the exact phraseology and wording that was used by his teachers. In this way, it was possible to study the Talmud from the written commentary in the absence of an instructor. Once a student mastered the talmudic text and style through the help of a teacher, he could then go on to study tractate after tractate, on his own, thanks to Rashi's commentary.

Though Rashi's work is a written crystallization of what was orally transmitted by the Franco-German academies, Rashi's original style, clarity, and erudition resulted in a superb and classic commentary on the Talmud.

To fully appreciate the importance of Rashi's commentary, one must look at the state and style of the text of the Babylonian Talmud. The *Mishnah* and Talmud, which comprise a major part of the Oral Law, were originally taught and transmitted orally. Finally, when the Oral Law was committed to writing, it was done in a manner that would preserve and retain its oral character. Thus, the talmudic text reads more like notations than a well-edited written codex. For this reason, it was almost impossible to study Talmud without the guidance of a talmudic master.

Just as in a speech, a comprehension of the speaker's words depends upon his tone of voice, pronunciation, gestures, and presentation. To properly understand the Talmud, one must receive training and guidance from a qualified pedagogue. Esra Shereshevsky states, "The Talmud could not reproduce the rhythm or the inflection of the speech of the Sages whose rulings it records; hence, each word in the Talmudic text can serve only as a cue for the student's memory. This written cue, if it is to have any meaning, must be 'reconstituted' into the spoken word."[10]

Rashi opened the Talmud to the student of Jewish lore and law. Without engaging in dialectics and mental gymnastics, Rashi determined the precise reading of the text and elucidated the words and terms of the Talmud. By verbally supplying the equivalent of modern punctuation marks, Rashi was able to eliminate certain difficulties. However, more than anything else, Rashi was sensitive to the mood as well as the logic of the Talmud. To this day one does not study "Talmud" or *Gemara* but "*Gemara* with Rashi." The well-known saying that "without Rashi, the Talmud would have been forgotten in Israel"[11] is no exaggeration.

THE TOSAFISTS

Copies of Rashi's commentary, called *kunteres* (pamphlets, because originally it was not written in book form but as separate pamphlets), were diligently studied in the various talmudic schools. In the course of study, detailed analytical discussions of Talmud and Rashi were carried out. The various commentaries, questions, and clarifications of the Franco-German scholars of the twelfth and thirteenth centuries are known as *Tosafot* (additions to Rashi's commentary). Many of the early Tosafists were Rashi's own sons-in-law (Rashi did not have any sons), grandsons, and great-grandsons. The style and approach of the Tosafists had great impact on the methods of all talmudic interpretation, especially in respect to the analytical school of talmudic exegesis.[12]

THE *ARUKH*: A TALMUDIC LEXICON

Another important work on the Talmud was composed by Rabbi Nathan ben Yehiel of Rome. Rabbi Nathan, living in the eleventh century, was the author of the classic talmudic lexicon entitled *Arukh*. More than a glossary of talmudic words and expressions, it is a talmudic encyclopedia that gives not only the meaning but also the etymology of talmudic terms. It embraces words of Aramaic, Latin, Greek, Arabic, and Persian origin. When defining a difficult term, Rabbi Nathan goes on to explain the passage in which that term is found. The *Arukh* is a rich source of geonic and Italian talmudic learning.[13] Soon after its appearance, it became a basic reference work for all talmudists, Ashkenazic as well as Sephardic. In modern times, the *Arukh* has been reedited and supplemented, but it still remains as a standard work in talmudic research.

The southern French medieval Jewish community of Provence also produced outstanding talmudic works.[14] A major achievement of talmudic scholarship was the work entitled *Bet ha-Behirah (The Chosen Abode)* by Rabbi Menahem ben Shlomo, ha-Meiri (1249–1316). It is a work written in a lucid Hebrew and combines the approaches of the Franco-German school with the Spanish school. It summarizes the subject matter of the Talmud by citing the *Mishnah* and then giving its meaning and the *halakhah* derived from it.

PILPUL

During the sixteenth century, various works on the Talmud were composed in eastern Europe, particularly in Poland, where Ashkenazic Jewry had been transplanted. The father of Torah study in Poland, Rabbi Jacob Pollack, was responsible for a new approach to talmudic study. His innovative method was a form of *pilpul* (dialectic) known as the *hiluk* (division and analysis). Meyer Waxman describes that method as follows:

> It consisted primarily in taking an apparently unified Talmudic subject and with fine analytic ability dissecting it into its component parts, drawing nice distinctions in their meaning, and then building up a new subject out of these newly defined parts. This method afforded ample room for mental ingenuity and hair splitting definitions which enchanted the young students.[15]

Many of the leading Talmud scholars of the period were opposed to the emphasis on *hiluk* and *pilpul,* and in their commentaries they stressed the more simple and analytical approaches of the Franco-German school. Some of the more important talmudic exegetes of this time were Rabbi Meir of Lublin, Rabbi Solomon Luria, and Rabbi Samuel Edels.

THE SUPERCOMMENTARIES OF MEIR OF LUBLIN, SOLOMON LURIA, AND SAMUEL EDELS

Rabbi Meir of Lublin, also known as Maharam, wrote glosses on the Talmud with special attention given to the clarification of Rashi and the *Tosafot*. His style is simple and clear. Rabbi Solomon Luria, in addition to doing the same as Rabbi Meir of Lublin, wrote *Yam Shel Shelomo (The Sea of Solomon)*, a code-commentary on seven tractates of the Babylonian Talmud. Maharshal, as Luria is sometimes called, was an independent thinker of extraordinary brilliance. Not only was he concerned with talmudic exegesis but he also established the correct text and readings of the Talmud. Many of Rabbi Luria's textual emendations were to appear in later printings of the Talmud.

Rabbi Samuel Edels, also known as Maharsha, wrote an exhaustive commentary on both the halakhic and aggadic portions of the Babylonian Talmud. Using the methodology of the Franco-German tosafists, Maharsha clarifies difficult passages in Rashi and *Tosafot*. His keenness of mind and rationalistic approach permeates his aggadic commentary as well.

Following in the footsteps of the tosafists, leading rabbinic scholars of the eighteenth century further refined and revolutionized the study of the Talmud. Such halakhists as Rabbi Akiva Eger, Rabbi Jacob of Lisa, and Rabbi Aryeh Leb ha-Kohen attempted to clarify the basic concepts relating to problems of the Talmud, with the actual question or law serving merely as a peg on which to hang the discussion. It must be remembered that in the Talmud itself there is very little abstraction of ideas and concepts. Instead, the Talmud employs models and case histories. These scholars of the eighteenth century attempted to explain the Talmud by means of defining and clarifying the basic halakhic concepts.

LITHUANIAN TALMUDISTS OF THE ANALYTICAL SCHOOL

These methods were further developed and perfected by the great Lithuanian talmudists of the analytical school, Rabbi Shimon Shkop (1860–1940) and Rabbi Hayyim Soloveitchik (1853–1918). Rabbi Soloveitchik, born in 1853 in the town of Volozhin, is considered the creator of a new trend in Talmud study. This method has been described as "a logical attempt to formulate more general abstract definitions of various talmudic problems by employing various legal distinctions . . . to explain different issues or reconcile conflicting statements."[16] Developing a suitable terminology with which to describe the different concepts, Rabbi Hayyim Soloveitchik demonstrated that the differences in the Talmud itself and of its interpreters stemmed from these differing concepts of law.[17]

To date, thousands of commentaries on the Talmud have been written. As a result, the study of the Talmud, without resorting to commentaries, is not only impractical but also inconceivable.

THE MODERN STUDY OF TALMUD

With the rise of the Wissenschaft des Judentums (Science of Judaism) movement in Germany in the nineteenth century, which advocated the study of Judaism by submitting it to critical and modern methods of research, the Talmud also came under critical analysis. Most of these "scientific" studies dealt with questions pertaining to the origin of talmudic literature and with the Talmud as a source of history. However, no real new commentary to the Talmud was produced by this school of thought. More recently, however, there have appeared a number of talmudic works of commentary and analysis employing both the classical approach and the techniques of modern literary criticism, with special emphasis on variant readings of the text.

The Talmud is printed in such a way that the *Mishnah* and *Gemara* are in the center of the page surrounded by various commentaries such as Rashi, *Tosafot,* Rabbenu Gershom, Rabbenu Hananel, Rabbi Akiva Eger, and others. It is as if the commentaries serve as the frame around the very text of the Talmud. Just as the frame of a picture tends to bring out the essence and creates a semblance of togetherness and completeness of the picture, so too the various commentaries—the framing of the Talmud—bring clarity and sharper focus to the meaning of the Talmud.

9
THE TALMUD ON TRIAL

Throughout history, the Talmud, one of the greatest creative accomplishments of the Jewish people, was banned, burned, and censored. Both from within and from without, and even before the Talmud was fully completed, numerous attempts were made to extinguish this spirit of Jewish creativity.

The rabbis of the *midrash* state:

> When the Holy One came to give the Torah, He told Moses in succession the Bible, *Mishnah, Aggadah,* and Talmud. Moses said unto Him: "Master of the World, write it for your children." He replied: "My wish is to give it to them in writing, but it is foreseen by Me that the nations of the world are destined to rule over them and to take it (the Oral Law) from them, and My children will be as the nations of the world. Therefore, the Bible give unto them in writing, and the *Mishnah, Aggadah* and Talmud orally."[1]

Thus, it is the Oral Law as embodied in the Talmud that renders the Jewish people unique. The definition of true Judaism, the real spirit of the Bible and its meaning, are all to be found in the Oral Law—the Talmud. Furthermore, from a sociohistorical standpoint no Jewish community could survive for long without the ability to study the Talmud. The study of the Talmud has, throughout the ages, given meaning and vitality to Jewish existence. In times of dire catastrophe and harsh persecution, the singsong *niggun* (the melody in which the Talmud was studied), the intricacies of talmudic dialectics, and the glowing warmth of the *aggadah* have all kept the Jewish spirit alive. It is this uniqueness and spirit that the enemies of the Jewish people tried to destroy in their attacks upon the Talmud.

The earliest attack on the Talmud goes back to the sixth century when Emperor Justinian attempted to strip Judaism of its legal rights. Among other things, the Justinian Code states, "But the *Mishnah,* or as they call it the second tradition, we prohibit entirely. For it is not part of the sacred books, nor is it handed down by divine inspiration through the prophets, but the handiwork of man, speaking only of earthly things and having nothing of the divine in it."[2] Justinian banned the study of the *Mishnah* for, according to him, it distorted the Bible and thereby hindered Christian missionary activities.

In the year 638 C.E., the Jews of Visigothic Spain were severely restricted in their observance of Jewish law, and a "declaration of faith" was exacted from the Jews of Toledo. Jews were to be sincere to the Christian faith, renounce all Jewish rites, eat everything that is eaten by Christians, marry only baptized Jews, and "hand over all Jewish books in their possession, including the Talmud. . . ."[3]

The most infamous trial and burning of the Talmud took place in France during the thirteenth century. A great dispute over the Talmud took place in Paris in 1240, and it was finally condemned to fire in the year 1242. This triggered a series of such incidents throughout Europe that influenced all subsequent anti-Semitic acts for centuries to come. Allan Temko, writing of the events of 1242, points out:

> The destruction of the Talmud was the beginning of a whole chain of disasters. A new law increased Jewish misery every two or three years until, in 1269, Saint Louis introduced the *rouelle,* "the little wheel," which the Jew would wear for five hundred years as a mark of humiliation. . . . Thus, while Western Europe was moving toward what we are pleased to call the Renaissance, the Jew was being dragged into a Dark Age. He would have little but tragedy until the French Revolution.[4]

A CHAIN OF DISASTERS

The litany is a long and sorrowful one. In Barcelona, in the year 1263, the Talmud was ordered burned. In 1264, Pope Clement IV decreed that any person caught with a copy of the Talmud in his possession be put to death. In 1299 and 1309, the Talmud was publicly burned in Paris. In 1322, by order of Pope John XXII, the Talmud was again publicly burned. Again in 1415, Pope Martin V ordered that all copies of the Talmud be destroyed. During the Spanish Inquisition in 1490, the infamous Torquemada ordered large-scale burning of the Talmud. In Germany, during the first half of the sixteenth century, the Dominican Order, instigated by the apostate Johannes Pfefferkorn, tried to have the Talmud destroyed. When the High Inquisitional Court established itself in Rome in 1542, there followed a series of public burnings of the Talmud. In 1544, Martin Luther, in his book *Concerning the Jews and their Lies,* described the Talmud as nothing but godlessness, lies, cursing, and swearing.[5] In 1553, Pope Julius III, in a papal bull, decreed that all books of the Talmud be burned. As a result, public burnings of the Talmud took place in Rome,

Bologna, Venice, Ferrara, Ancona, and Montoba. Similar incidents occurred in Holland in 1559 and Poland in 1757.

This anti-Talmud sentiment continued into modern times. At the end of the seventeenth century, Johann Andreas Eisenmenger (1654–1704), a German Protestant professor, published the infamous *Jewry Unmasked,* which was subtitled "An Original and True Account of the Way in Which the Stubborn Jews Frightfully Blaspheme and Dishonor the Holy Trinity, Revile the Holy Mother of Christ, Mockingly Criticize the New Testament, the Evangelists, the Apostles and the Christian Religion, and Despise and Curse to the Uttermost Extreme the Whole of Christianity." Eisenmenger's work was to serve as a fountainhead for a vast network of anti-Talmud and anti-Semitic literature.

Toward the end of the nineteenth century, August Rohling (1839–1931), professor of Hebrew Antiquities at Prague, published the *Talmud Jew.* This volume, mostly a rehashing of Eisenmenger's *Jewry Unmasked,* went through seventeen editions with a circulation of two hundred thousand copies in Austria alone.

In 1892, Justin Pranaitis published his book *The Christian in the Jewish Talmud* in St. Petersburg. In 1912, during the trial of Mendel Beilis, who was accused of ritual murder, Pranaitis volunteered his services and talmudic "expertise" to the czarist government and tried to show that Beilis was guilty of ritual murder "by reason of Talmudic teachings."[6]

In Nazi Germany, anti-Talmud propaganda was written by Walter Forstat under the title *The Basic Principles of the Talmud* and by Alfred Rosenberg, a friend and associate of Hitler, in his book *Immorality in the Talmud.*

THE DEBATE OF 1240

From a historical perspective, the various incidents resulting in the burning of the Talmud and the vast anti-Talmud propaganda are all rooted in the great disputation of 1240 in France. The arguments presented at this debate were to be reiterated and rehashed time and time again. Therefore, to better understand this anti-Talmud attitude, it is necessary to study the arguments, pro and con, of that historic disputation.

Nicholas Donin, a rabbinic student, was excommunicated by his teacher for his heretical views. Upon turning apostate and seeking revenge against his former coreligionists, in 1240 Donin presented a formal accusation against the Talmud to Pope Gregory IX. Donin made extracts from the Talmud and formulated thirty-five articles on which he based his charges. The essence of these allegations were that (1) the Talmud is the source of the Jewish "stiff-neckedness" and it alone is the cause of Jews stubbornly refusing to accept Christianity; (2) the great importance attached to the Talmud by the Jews is an affront to the Bible and Prophets; and (3) the Talmud contains blasphemies against God, Jesus, and the Christian religion.

On receipt of Donin's accusations, transcripts of the apostate's articles were dispatched by Gregory to the heads of church in France, England, Spain, and Portugal. Orders to confiscate all copies of the Talmud and begin an investigation of its contents were zealously carried out in France. A public disputation was scheduled. Nicholas Donin and Eudes de Chateauroux, chancellor of the Sorbonne, represented the Christian side. Four leading rabbis who defended the Talmud and Judaism were Yehiel of Paris, the leading rabbi of France, Moshe of Coucy, Yehudah ben David of Melun, and Shmuel ben Shlomo of Chateau-Thiery. They were all of the famed tosafist school, which flourished in France and Germany in the twelfth to fourteenth centuries and contributed valuable *tosafot* (additions) to Talmud commentaries. Queen Blanche, mother of King Louis IX, named herself chief judge. After three days of debate, it was decided that the royal court was not best qualified to judge such theological matters. The disputation was then transferred to a church tribunal. The clerics did not

reach an immediate decision, and only after further delibera-
tions did they issue their verdict: the Talmud was condemned
as a "tissue of lies"[7] and sentenced to be destroyed by fire.

THE PUBLIC BURNING OF THE TALMUD

The sentence of condemnation remained unexecuted for a few
years. The Archbishop of Sens, a member of the church tribunal, interceded on behalf of the Jews and prevented the sentence from being carried out. However, the friendly archbishop suddenly died. This was viewed by the fanatical
elements in the Church as a heaven-sent punishment for his
having befriended the Jews. Shortly thereafter, on the first
Sabbath of Lent in the year 1242, while the Jews were assem-
bled in their synagogues, twenty-four cartloads of thousands
of Talmud manuscripts were carried off and publicly put to the
torch.

There exist two accounts of the disputation about the
Talmud that took place in Paris in the year 1240. There is a
Hebrew version entitled *Vikuah Rabbenu Yehiel mi-Paris* ("The
Disputation of Rabbi Yehiel of Paris")[8] that was probably
compiled by the rabbi's students. There is also a Latin source
entitled *Extractiones de Talmut.*[9] Careful examination of these
two sources reveals that there were basically two charges
brought against the Talmud. First, it was charged that the
Talmud was the source of all errors the Church charged
against the Jews and Judaism. Second, it was alleged that the
Talmud contained blasphemies against Christianity.

Concerning the first point, the Church and Donin acted in a
subtle manner. They accused the Talmud of being an insult to
the Bible inasmuch as the Jews attach far too much importance
to the Talmud. In Donin's "Thirty-five Articles," the first
nine articles concentrate on this issue and severely attack the

Oral Law. In reaction to Donin's accusations, Pope Gregory stated in an official communication:

> For they (the Jews), so we have heard, are not content with the old law which God gave Moses in writing, they even ignore it completely, and affirm that God gave another law which is called "Talmud," that is "teaching," handed down to Moses orally. Falsely they allege that it was implanted within their minds and unwritten, was there preserved until certain men came, whom they call Sages and Scribes, who fearing that this law may be lost . . . reduced it to writing, and the volume of this by far exceeds the text of the Bible.[10]

The exact motives behind the apostate Donin's severe criticisms of the Oral Law are unclear. Some historians maintain that Donin was a Karaite[11] (a member of the medieval Jewish splinter-sect who strongly denied the authenticity of the Oral Law), and for this reason he was bitter and antagonistic toward the Talmud—a reason that had little to do with its allegedly being anti-Christian. Others see in Donin's attack pure revenge against the rabbis who previously had rejected and excommunicated him in the year 1225.[12]

No doubt, the Catholic church's vehement attack on the Oral Law was rooted in its efforts to convert Jews to Christianity. The Church felt that if not for the Talmud, the way to mass Jewish conversion would be wide open. By accusing the Jews of giving more attention and attaching more importance to the Talmud than to the Bible and Prophets, the Church attempted to bring down from around the Jews the very source of their traditional separatism. Such thinking is strongly hinted at in a papal letter of Pope Innocent IV to the King of France that read in part, "But of the laws and doctrines of the Prophets they make their sons altogether ignorant. They fear that if the forbidden truth, which is found in the Law and the Prophets, be understood . . . their children would be converted to the faith and humbly return to their redeemer."[13]

It must be borne in mind that according to Christian doctrine, the Hebrew Bible is a prefiguration of their New Testament, which contains the Christ story. Many passages of the Hebrew Bible are given as proof texts of various aspects of this story. Hence the pope's reference to the "forbidden truth" in the Bible that the Jews allegedly feared.

In Defense of the Talmud

Concerning Donin's second charge that the Talmud contains blasphemies against Christianity, the Church compiled a list of talmudic statements regarding Jesus and Gentiles *(goyim)* that they considered offensive. The Jewish rejoinder to these accusations, as recorded in the *Vikuah Rabbenu Yehiel mi-Paris,* is that there exists a distinction between contemporary Gentiles and those living in talmudic times. "Take this as a rule," says Rabbi Yehiel, "wherever the word *goy* is mentioned in the Talmud, it refers to a member of one of the seven nations who made peace by accepting the condition of paying tribute."[14] The logic of this defense is interesting. By falling back from the Talmud to the Bible, the Jew gained common ground with his Christian opponent. As Jacob Katz writes, "If the disqualification of Gentiles mentioned in the Talmud applied to the 'Seven Nations' of Palestine, the blame for it, if blame is due, attached not only to those who adhered to the Talmud, but also to all who shared the belief in the divine origin of the Bible."[15]

Similarly, any derogatory statement in the Talmud about Jesus does not refer to Jesus, the Christian Savior, but to someone else by that name—a name not uncommon during the Second Temple period. Whether these arguments of defense were genuine views or simply a polemic device used in the course of debate is not at all clear.

Though Donin's exposé of the Talmud leaves one with the impression that the Talmud is full of anti-Christian hatred and venom, actually there is very little, if any, reference to Christianity in the Talmud. Edward Flannery points out, "Its 'conspiracy of silence' regarding Christianity has been noted. Theologian of Orthodoxy F. Lovsky is quite right when he writes that, 'on the whole, the Talmud sins much more by an evidently well guarded silence with respect to Christianity than by tendentious insults or accusations.' "[16]

THE PFEFFERKORN-REUCHLIN CONTROVERSY

Another important trial of the Talmud took place in the sixteenth century in Germany. With the advent of printing, copies of the Hebrew Bible and Talmud circulated throughout Europe. Johannes Pfefferkorn, a butcher by profession, converted to Christianity at the age of thirty-six, with his wife and children. Living in Cologne under the protection of the Dominican Order, Pfefferkorn wrote numerous anti-Semitic books. Alarmed by the wide circulation given the Talmud, Pfefferkorn called for its suppression. With the support of the Dominicans and the help of Kunigunde, Emperor Maximilian's sister, Pfefferkorn obtained permission to confiscate any offensive Jewish books. The Talmud was high on his list. When Pfefferkorn encountered strong opposition from the archbishop of Mainz, the Frankfort City Council, and members of the German nobility, the emperor ordered that the confiscated tomes be returned. Six weeks later, under pressure from his sister and due to an alleged blood libel and host desecration at Bradenberg, the emperor appointed a commission to investigate Pfefferkorn's charges against the Talmud.

Serving on this committee, which was chaired by the archbishop of Mainz, was the noted scholar and leading humanist

Johannes Reuchlin. Reuchlin, a Christian scholar and Hebraist, was visited by Pfefferkorn in 1510. Pfefferkorn asked him to assist in the confiscation of the Talmud. Reuchlin refused to have any part in this, and only by imperial order did he consent to serve on the commission.

The Christian humanist and admirer of Jewish scholarship defended the Talmud against Pfefferkorn's accusations. Regarding Pfefferkorn, Reuchlin wrote, "The Talmud was not composed for every blackguard to trample with unwashed feet and then to say he knew all of it."[17] Fellow German humanists supported Reuchlin, including Erasmus, who termed Pfefferkorn "a criminal Jew who had become a most criminal Christian."[18] What followed was a bitter battle between the Reuchlinists and the anti-Reuchlinists. Reuchlin was accused of heresy and was cited before the Inquisition. Only after standing trial before an ecclesiastical tribunal in the city of Speyer was Reuchlin acquitted of all charges.

These sordid events not only witnessed the sparing of the Talmud but they also resulted in a decline of the prestige of the Church. Indeed, it is no mere coincidence that Martin Luther launched the Reformation in 1517—at the very height of the Pfefferkorn-Reuchlin controversy.

CENSORSHIP

Even when the Talmud was not condemned to fire, it was still mutilated at the hands of the censors. When Pope Pius IV announced in 1564 that the Talmud could be circulated, it was on condition that those parts that offended Christians be deleted. Consequently, when the Talmud, with such deletions, was printed in Basel between 1578 and 1581, it bore the imprimatur, or official sanction, of the Catholic church. The censored Basel edition of the Babylonian Talmud served as a model for subsequent editions. Father Marco Marino, the

Basel censor, even deleted the word *Talmud* replacing it with *Gemara* or *Shas* (an abbreviation of the Hebrew *Shishah Sedarim*—the six orders of the *Mishnah*). References to Rome were changed to read Aram (Mesopotamia) or Paras (Persia). The Hebrew word *min* (heretic) was changed by Marino to read Sadducee or Epicurean. Words such as *mumar* (apostate) and *goy* (Gentile) were eliminated or changed. In the Basel edition, the censor replaced the term *goy* with the word *kushi* (African)! Of course, all references to the name *Jesus* were deleted, and the whole tractate *Avodah Zarah,* which deals with paganism and Jewish relations with non-Jews, was not printed at all. The Basel censor went so far as to change sections he personally regarded as offensive. Thus, the talmudic saying that "a man who has no wife cannot be called a man,"[19] which obviously insulted Father Marino's sensibilities as a celibate, was changed to read, "A Jew who has no wife cannot be called a man."[20]

Why was the Talmud singled out and made the constant target of anti-Semites throughout the ages? Perhaps the "mystique" of the Talmud and its overpowering dialectical style gave rise to suspicion in the minds of the unknowing. Or perhaps it was because the talmudic way of life was regarded as an obstacle to the conversion of the Jews to Christianity. The Talmud, its study, and the observance of its laws set the Jews apart from their Christian neighbors. Edward Flannery aptly says, "The Talmud served the cause of anti-Semitism indirectly insofar as it reinforced Israel's traditional separatism."[21]

Whatever the case may be, the Talmud, like the Jewish People, has survived the trials and tribulations of the ages.

10

RELIGIOUS IDEAS OF TALMUDIC JUDAISM

It should be understood that the rabbis of the Talmud were not philosophers in the Western sense. One should not expect to find in the Talmud any complete homogenous treatise on philosophical issues. Yet, an abundance of philosophical and theological material is scattered throughout the pages of the Talmud in the form of biblical commentary, legal decisions, anecdotes, parables, and even prayers. To obtain a clear picture of talmudic thought, it is necessary to carefully analyze the text and to extract from it the thinking of the rabbis on particular religious and philosophical questions. Ephraim Urbach, in commenting on the difficulty of this task, states:

> Common to all the sources is the fact that none of them provides systematic treatment of the subject of beliefs and conceptions, and there are almost no continuous discourses dealing with a single theme. In most instances we have to integrate and arrange the scattered material into one unit of thought. A great fund of terms and concepts was created in the era of the Sages, some of which are not known—at least in their present formulation—in the

Bible, and some, although found in Scripture, have acquired a different meaning and content.[1]

Because of these and similar difficulties, there is a tendency on the part of many authors to read into the talmudic text their own system of ideas. Thus, medieval Jewish philosophers, mystics, expounders of hasidic thought, and Jewish existentialists all base themselves on talmudic texts and views. In the course of time, only a handful of scholars have treated the beliefs and ideas of the rabbis against the background of their times and environment. The most recent work of this type is *The Sages: Their Concepts and Beliefs* by Ephraim Urbach.

GREEK THOUGHT AND THE TALMUD

A question frequently asked concerning the philosophy of the talmudic sages is whether or not they were familiar with and influenced by Greek philosophical thought.

Yitzhak Baer, a noted Israeli historian writing some thirty years ago, maintained that the rabbis of the Talmud were strongly influenced by Platonic ideas.[2] However, Baer's thesis has been challenged by Saul Lieberman, who claims that there is no evidence that the rabbis were familiar with formal philosophy.[3] The talmudic sages never once mention Plato, Aristotle, or the Stoics. Similarly, writes Lieberman, "Greek philosophic terms are absent from the entire ancient Rabbinic literature."[4] Lieberman does concede to Baer that "some elements of Greek philosophy penetrated into Palestinian Rabbinic circles."[5] However, unlike Baer, Lieberman is not prepared to say that "the Rabbis were strongly influenced by Platonic ideas, and that Rabbinic methods of interpretation were directly affected by the dialectics of the Greek philosophical school."[6]

GOD'S TRANSCENDENCE AND IMMANENCE

An interesting dichotomy exists in the talmudic conception of God. On the one hand, the rabbis stress the transcendence of God. God is spoken of as being far off in heaven, exalted, mighty, and majestic. This notion tends to create a wide chasm between man and God. Indeed, a talmudic euphemism for God is *Shamayim* (Heaven).[7] On the other hand, the Talmud views God as inhabiting the "world below," His presence filling the whole universe. God is called by the rabbis *ha-Makom* (the Omnipresent).[8]

This dichotomy of nearness and distance, transcendence and immanence is set forth in the *Shemonah Esrei* prayer (the eighteen benedictions) that is recited three times a day by the devout Jew. In this prayer, of talmudic origin, these dual qualities of God are emphasized:

> Blessed are You, Lord our God and God of our fathers, God of Abraham, God of Isaac and God of Jacob; great, mighty and revered God, sublime God, who bestows lovingkindness, and the Master of all things; who remembers the good deeds of our fathers. . . . You are mighty forever, my Master; You are the resurrector of the dead, the powerful One to deliver us. Sustainer of the living with kindness, resurrector of the dead with great mercy, supporter of the fallen, and healer of the sick, and releaser of the imprisoned. . . .[9]

In this prayer, the Jew bridges heaven and earth. God, who is great, sublime, mighty, and revered is also the personal God of Abraham, Isaac, and Jacob. He supports the fallen, heals the sick, and releases the imprisoned. The omnipresence of God characterizes Him as a personal God, a God whose abode is high in the heavens, but at the same time He is personally concerned with man. This concept of a personal God is the very basis for many rituals and practices in Rabbinic Judaism.

Prayer, according to the Talmud, is not only praise and glorification of the Almighty; it is also *bakashah* (petitional). Man beseeches God and seeks His help and counsel, knowing that God is listening.

This closeness man feels toward God is poignantly brought out in the following story:

It happened once that there was a terrible drought in the land of Israel. Honi ha-Ma'agel—Honi the Circle Maker, (who was a famous miracle worker of the Second Temple period) was asked to pray that rain should fall. He did so, but rain did not fall. He then drew a circle and placed himself in its center . . . and said before God: "Master of the World! Your children have set their face upon me, because I am, as it were, Your intimate. I swear by Your great name that I will not move from here until You show mercy to Your children." Rain began to trickle. . . . Thereupon Honi spoke again: "Not for such rain did I pray, but for rain sufficient to fill the cisterns, ditches and caves." The rain came down with vehemence, each drop as big as the opening of a barrel. . . . Again Honi spoke: "Not for such rain did I pray, but for a rain of benevolence, blessing and graciousness!" The rain then continued in proper measure so that the Israelites had to go up from the (flooded) streets of Jerusalem to the Temple Mount (high ground) on account of the rain. The people then said to Honi: "Just as you prayed for the rain to come, so pray now that it should stop. . . ." Thereupon, Honi prayed and said: "Master of the World! Your people Israel, whom You have brought out of Egypt, can stand neither too much good, nor too much punishment: when You became angry with them and withheld the rain, they could not stand it, and now that You showered much good upon them, they again cannot stand it; let it be Your will that there be ease in the world." Immediately the wind blew, the clouds dispersed and the sun began to shine. . . .[10]

This charming but somewhat dramatic story emphasizes the closeness and familiarity the Jew feels toward God. Honi ha-Ma'agel considered himself on intimate terms with God.

When God did not answer his prayers, he refused to move from the spot, insisting that the Lord heed his plea. When God did not send the kind of rain requested, Honi argued with the Almighty.

Such fundamental concepts of talmudic thought about reward, punishment, and repentance make sense only in terms of God's omnipresence and closeness to man. The *Mishnah* in *Avot* teaches, "Mark well three things and you shall not fall into the clutches of sin: Know what is above you—an eye that sees, an ear that hears, and all your actions are recorded in the book."[11] Of course, the eye, ear, and book are figures of speech, but they concretely stress God's concern and involvement with the actions of man. Furthermore, because of man's intimacy with God, there is no need for a mediator. "If a man is in distress," says the Talmud, "let him not call on the angels Michael or Gabriel, but let him call directly on God and He will hearken to him straightaway."[12]

In stressing God's transcendence and immanence, the Talmud calls God *Shekhinah* (dwelling) and expresses the idea that God manifests Himself on the stage of the world although dwelling in the highest of heavens. The *midrash* teaches that "when Israel went down to Egypt, *Shekhinah* went down with them; when they came up from Egypt, *Shekhinah* came up with them; whenever Israel is enslaved, *Shekhinah*, as it were, is enslaved with them."[13]

The nearness and distance of God in rabbinic thought was not always fully understood; and in the opinion of some, the dichotomy of immanence and transcendence was suggestive of dualism. The following encounter between the talmudic sage Rabban Gamliel and a heretic is recorded in the Talmud:

A heretic said to Rabban Gamliel: "You Rabbis declare that wherever ten people assemble for worship, the *Shekhinah* abides among them; how many *Shekhinahs* are there then?" Rabban Gamliel called the (heretic's) servant and tapped him on the neck, saying, "Why does the sun enter into your master's house?" "But," he exclaimed, "the sun shines upon the whole world!" "Then if the sun, which is only one out of the countless myriads of God's servants, shines on the whole world, how much more so the *Shekhinah* of the Holy One, blessed be He, Himself."[14]

God's nearness to man also emphasizes the notion that God is not merely the God of creation but the God of history as well. God speaks through historical events. He redeems Israel from slavery in Egypt, He reveals His law to Israel. And He will, at some point in the future, bring universal salvation unto mankind. Of course, this nearness is determined by man's behavior and knowledge of God.[15]

FREE WILL VERSUS DIVINE PROVIDENCE

Another area of talmudic thought in which seemingly opposing or contradictory ideas coexist is that of free will versus divine providence. Basic to the talmudic outlook was the doctrine of freedom of the will, that man is free to choose between good and evil. A system of reward and punishment can be operative only within a scheme of free will. On the other hand, great emphasis is placed on the fact that all that occurs on earth is due to divine intervention and is predetermined. Talmudic literature abounds with comments such as, "No man can touch that which has been prepared in advance for his friend"[16]; "No man bruises his finger here on earth unless it was so decreed against him in heaven"[17]; "Forty days before a child is formed a heavenly voice decrees, so and so's daughter shall marry so and so"[18]; "Everything is in the hands of heaven except cold and heat"[19]; and "All is in the hand of heaven except the fear of heaven."[20]

The tension between the doctrine of free will and divine

providence was frequently noted by the Talmud.[21] Steven Katz correctly remarks:

> The combination of these two doctrines within rabbinic theology may be understood, not so much from the philosophical point of view, but rather from the practical point of view which underlies all rabbinic thinking. On the one hand it is necessary to think of the world as under the complete surveillance and control of heaven, a thought which adds to the confidence and trust of the Jew in God, and on the other hand the individual needs to make his choices and decisions on the assumption that evil and good are both within his grasp. The conceptual integration of these two ideas did not enter rabbinic thought forms.[22]

Maimonides, the great twelfth-century talmudist and philosopher, did attempt to ease the tension of these two doctrines. Basing himself on the saying of Rabbi Akiva that "everything is foreseen, but freedom of choice is given," Maimonides posits that though God has foreknowledge of all acts, man's freedom is not limited, and all that happens is man's own choice.[23]

IMITATIO DEI: EMULATING GOD

An important belief concerning both God and man stressed by the sages of the Talmud is the concept of *imitatio dei* (the imitating of God). Actually, the principle of *imitatio dei* is found in the Bible. Man created in the image of God is endowed with a superior status that enables him to "copy" the ways of God. The rabbis of the Talmud, in their discussions of *imitatio dei,* stress the fact that it is only in conduct and not in terms of essence that man is to imitate God. Thus, we are enjoined to be holy, "for holy am I the Lord your God." In other words, one can achieve a certain holiness in behavior and conduct but not holiness in essence.

In striving to emulate the ways of God, man must always remember his place: "Israel" says Abba Saul, a third-century teacher, "are the household servants of the King, and it is incumbent upon them to imitate the King."[24] Just as the servant who walks in the footsteps of his master, emulating the ways of his superior, must always be cognizant that he is only a servant, so too, when walking in the ways of God, man must remember that after all he is only mortal man.

Commenting on the verse, "After the Lord your God you shall walk,"[25] the talmudic sage Rabbi Hama, son of Rabbi Hanina, asked:

> How can man walk after God? Is He not a consuming fire? What is meant is that man ought to walk after, that is, imitate the attributes of God. Just as the Lord clothes the naked, so you shall clothe the naked. Just as He visits the sick, so you shall visit the sick. Just as the Lord comforted the bereaved, so you shall also comfort the bereaved. Just as He buried the dead, so too you shall bury the dead.[26]

God serves as a model for man's behavior. But how far does this go? For is not God also a God of stern justice, jealous and vengeful of the wicked? Are we to imitate these qualities as well? The rabbis of the Talmud limited the application of *imitatio dei* only to the qualities of divine mercy. God alone knows how to best employ the four attributes of jealousy, vengeance, exaltation, and circuity. Man cannot be trusted with such qualities, lest he become obsessed with them.

Underlying the principle of *imitatio dei* is the concept that not only are the actions of God ideals for human conduct but that God, unlike human rulers and other deities, does not reserve all the glory and qualities of divinity for Himself. The Talmud stresses that God is most eager and willing to share these ideal qualities with all those created in His image.

One of the highest spiritual achievements attainable by man, as viewed by the Talmud, is the attainment of *kedushah* (a state of holiness). Rabbi Pinhas ben Yair states:

> The knowledge of Torah leads to watchfulness, watchfulness to zeal, zeal to cleanliness, cleanliness to abstinence, abstinence to purity, purity to saintliness, saintliness to humility, humility to the fear of sin, and the fear of sin to holiness.[27]

KEDUSHAH: HOLINESS

Man is called on to be holy and thus emulate God, who is holy. In fact, in rabbinic literature, God is frequently called by the name *ha-Kadosh Barukh Hu,* the Holy One, Blessed Be He.[28] What exactly is *kedushah*? The talmudic teachers explain the biblical verse, "You shall be holy . . ." by stating, "You shall be separated."[29] This separation *(perishut)* is frequently equated with abstinence from illicit sexual relations, idolatry, and general immorality and lewd behavior. Thus, "separation" as understood by the Talmud is not to be taken in the metaphysical sense of aloofness or withdrawal but as a physical separation from impure and defiling things. Commenting on the verse, "And you shall be unto Me a kingdom of priests and a holy nation,"[30] the sages states, "Be unto Me a kingdom of priests, separated from the nations of the world and their abominations."[31]

Holiness, in a more positive vein, is attained when the Jew performs the commandments of the Torah. The holiness of God is absolute and is not dependent on man: "For I am holy, I abide in My holiness whether you hallow Me or not."[32] But man's attainment of holiness depends upon his own behavior. Man must sanctify himself, and this he can achieve only by the observance of God's laws as embodied in the Torah. Thus, when one is about to perform a *mitzvah* (a commandment) and recites the appropriate benediction, he states, "Blessed are You the Lord our God, King of the universe, who sanctifies us with His commandments. . . ."

However, the concept of *holiness* goes beyond these technical aspects of separation and performance. *Kedushah* manifests itself in three particular realms: space, time, and spirit. When the Talmud speaks about the holiness of space *(kedushat ha-makom)*, it is referring to the phenomenon of specific places and of inanimate things that have attained a degree of holiness. Thus, the *Mishnah* teaches that "there are ten ascending degrees of holiness," beginning with the land of Israel and extending to the Holy of Holies in the Temple at Jerusalem.[33] Similarly, objects serving a sacred purpose, such as Torah scrolls, holy writings, synagogue buildings, and so forth, possess varying degrees of holiness and can only be exchanged for objects having a higher sanctity.[34]

Holiness in time *(kedushat ha-zeman)* are those periods of time, such as the Sabbath, the Festivals, and the Sabbatical and Jubilee years, that have been designated as holy times. And finally, holiness of spirit is both the individual and collective consecration of the Jewish people by God.

The concept of *holiness* as manifested in these three areas suggests that essentially the whole world, in all dimensions, has been endowed with the potentiality of holiness. *Kedushah* is then, as originally defined, not just a separation but a consecration. The talmudic concept of *holiness* calls upon man to consecrate the seemingly secular and mundane. Thus, for example, the human consumption of food, when performed in accordance with halakhic etiquette, is raised from a mere biological function to a sublime and holy ritual. The rabbis often compared the dining table to the holy altar of the Temple.[35] By associating all the various realms—space, time, and spirit—with goodness and purity, their full potential is attained and thereby perfected and made holy.

Asceticism

The separation and abstinence associated with holiness should not be misconstrued as a form of asceticism. The Talmud is opposed to all forms of asceticism and monasticism. Statements such as, "A person is forbidden to torture himself" and "One who engages in fasting (for self-affliction) is called a sinner,"[36] were common among the talmudic sages. Commenting on the fact that a Nazarite must make atonement upon the termination of his Nazarite vow, the Talmud states, "It can only mean that he denied himself the enjoyment of wine. Now, if a person who denies himself the enjoyment of wine is called a sinner, all the more so one who denies himself all the enjoyment of life."[37]

Kedushah manifests itself within man's natural life. Man is not expected to deny himself any of his physical, economic, or social needs. What the concept of *kedushah* stresses is the converting or transmuting of the natural and physical into the sublime and pure. As emphasized before, the means to *kedushah* is the *halakhah;* it guides man toward his ultimate sanctity without denying him his natural existence. *Kedushah* is not necessarily a mystical experience. Rather, it is a quality that is directed to the natural and practical aspects of life and far from a separate, independent kind of human experience. *Kedushah* is an act of dedication or perfection of time, space, and spirit through a withdrawal from all that is impure and defiling, whereby these realms attain their highest possible fulfillment.[38]

Ethical Conduct as a Divine Imperative

Ethical behavior is generally perceived to be a voluntary action on the part of man. According to this view, man "ought" to act in an ethical or "good" fashion because he feels that such behavior is morally and rationally correct. However, the Bible—when speaking of good and evil, right and wrong—does not seem to view such conduct as totally dependent upon the voluntary actions of mankind. To be good and do right as well as to perform acts of kindness are forms of behavior required of man by God. Hence, in Judaism the line that divides ethics from law is really rather thin. Menachem Marc Kellner states, ". . . the all embracing character of Jewish law would seem to leave no room for supralegal Jewish ethics as such. To characterize Jewish ethics simply, we may say that it attempts to show what Judaism, either in the guise of halakhah, or in some other form, teaches about moral issues."[39]

Though it would seem that modes of ethical conduct are divine imperatives, the rabbis of the Talmud do view the rules pertaining to them as distinct from other divine imperatives. In rabbinic literature, a definite distinction is drawn between those laws relating to matters between man and man and those between man and God. When one sins and disobeys the ethical commandments—that is, the code of human conduct governing relations between man and man—he is not only sinning against God by disobeying the divine will, but he sins against his fellowman as well. To receive atonement for mistreating one's fellow human being, it is therefore not enough to merely ask for forgiveness from God. The Talmud teaches, "For transgressions as between man and his fellow the Day of Atonement does not procure any atonement until he has pacified his fellow."[40] Even on the Day of Atonement (Yom Kippur), the holiest day of the year, a day when sins are forgiven and atonement secured, if one fails to apologize and make amends to his fellowman for acts of misbehavior, "the Day of Atonement does not procure for him any atonement."

Another interesting point made by the talmudic sages concerning the so-called ethical commandments is the fact that unlike many of the ritual laws that concern behavior between man and God, those between man and man are amenable to rational explanation. In an interesting talmudic passage, the rabbis show that there exists a category of ethical behavior outside of the Sinaitic revelation:

> Our rabbis taught: "Mine ordinances shall you do."[41] Such commandments which, if not written in Scripture, should by right have been written. They are: The laws concerning idolatry, immorality, bloodshed, robbery and blasphemy.[42]

Though all ethical laws are of divine origin, the rabbis stress that many of these revealed laws are completely rational and are accepted by mankind voluntarily. Not to murder or steal, for example, are rationalistic injunctions. Irrespective of their revelational character, they are voluntarily followed by society.

If this is so, why then is there the need for a divine imperative? The necessity for such imperatives is explained by the Talmud in the following manner: "He who is commanded and fulfills the command is greater than he who fulfills it though not commanded."[43] The logic of this statement seems somewhat askew, for if one is not enjoined to carry out a specific duty and nevertheless does so voluntarily, should he not receive the greater reward for such zeal and initiative? However, the Talmud is stressing the fact that psychologically speaking, the temptation to transgress an imperative exists in a situation of superimposed obligations. When one has to do something, there is frequently the urge to try not to do it. Thus, according to the Talmud, when one overpowers the temptation to resist a commandment and nevertheless performs the deed, he is entitled to a greater reward than he who fulfills a good deed without having to overcome any real challenge.[44]

Although the ethical laws of the Torah do not really require God's injunction as manifested in the revelation at Sinai, in fact almost half of the Ten Commandments fall into the ethical category. According to the talmudic teacher Rabbi Hananiah ben Akashya, "the Holy One, Blessed is He, wished to enable the people of Israel to acquire merit; therefore He gave them a super-abundant Torah and a multitude of *mitzvot*."[45]

THE LEGAL CHARACTER OF ETHICS

Since in the biblical and talmudic accounts the ethical laws of behavior are rooted in divine imperatives and are not left to man's good sense, it is natural that ethics takes on a legalistic character. The standard form of correct behavior, such as visiting the sick, helping the poor, consoling the bereaved, and so forth, bear a definite legal stamp. In the halakhic scheme, almsgiving and acts of kindness are treated as legal obligations, subject to the numerous concepts and rules of talmudic jurisprudence. For example, the Talmud declares that one must reside in a town thirty days before becoming liable for contributing to the soup kitchen and three months for the charity box.[46] The Talmud prescribes what percent of one's income should go to charity[47]; the act of pledging to charity is conceptually viewed as a vow[48]; and according to some opinions, charity is subject to compulsory assessment and collection.[49] Thus, an act that is generally based on one's moral conscience is carefully spelled out in law.

To avoid reducing acts of loving-kindness to obligatory, informal, or routine performances, the rabbis of the Talmud insisted that a large measure of subjectivity be present in the performance of such acts. Emphasis is placed on the inward experience as well. It is not enough to simply write out a check for the needy. The donor is enjoined to treat the recipient with respect and dignity, with patience and understanding. The Talmud teaches that "if a man were to give his fellow all the good gifts in the world but his face is sullen, it is ascribed to him as though he had given him nothing; but he who receives his fellow with a cheerful countenance, even if he gave him nothing, it is ascribed to him as though he had given him all the good gifts in the world."[50]

Thus, the talmudic view of social ethics is a synthesis of letter and spirit. Isadore Twersky writes:

> The halakhah undertook to convert an initially amorphous, possibly even capricious act into a rigidly defined and totally regulated performance. . . . However, while objectifying and concretizing a subjective, fluid state of mind, it insisted relentlessly upon the proper attitude, feeling, and manner of action.[51]

In the area of social ethics, the halakhic approach has thus transformed that which is generally considered voluntary in nature into a legal obligation. By not allowing social ethics to be subject to man's passing moods and whims, the *halakhah* has guaranteed that social and moral law will prevail and thereby prevent the world from turning into a sophisticated jungle of instincts and impulses.

HUMAN DIGNITY

High on the scale of talmudic values is the principle of human dignity *(kavod ha-briyot)*. Since man is created in God's image, the rabbis of the Talmud stressed that when one insults a fellow human being, he is insulting one created in the image of God.[52] Acts of indignity and humiliation to one's fellowman are cardinal sins akin to murder: "A *tanna* recited before Rabbi Nahman b. Yitzhak: He who publicly shames his neighbor is as though he shed blood."[53] According to talmudic law, compensation for wounds inflicted upon one's fellowman must also include payment for the indignity inflicted.[54]

Dignity of man is so basic to the talmudic ethical scheme

that it even supersedes a rabbinic commandment. Thus, in order to maintain human dignity, one is allowed to carry a dead body from a public domain to a semiprivate domain *(karmelit)*, even on the Sabbath.[55]

The basis for human dignity is the idea that man is created in the image of God, and it is concerning this that the *midrash* comments upon the verse in Exodus:

> Neither shall you go by the steps into mine altar, that your nakedness be not uncovered thereon.[56] It is *a fortiori*—if in regard to stones we have to be careful not to show any disrespect to them, then in the case of your fellowman who is made in the image of your creator, who is particular about any disrespect shown to Him, how much more certain is it that you should not treat him disrespectfully.[57]

Indeed, one may rightfully say that the principle of "inalienable rights" is rooted in talmudic ethics as a basic expression of "in the image of God He created man."

EXTRA-CREDIT MORALITY

Thus far, we have taken the position that the source for ethical and proper behavior is the *halakhah*. However, there are a number of talmudic texts that at first glance seem to suggest that there exist nonlegal or suprahalakhic moral considerations as well.

Commenting on the verse, "And you shall show them the way they must walk therein and the work that they shall do,"[58] the Talmud states:

> For Rabbi Yosef taught: "And you shall show them"—this refers to their house of life (interpreted to mean either the study of Torah or a trade from which one derives a livelihood); "the way"—that

means the practice of loving deeds; "they must walk"—to visit the sick; "therein"—to burial (of the poor who cannot pay for it); "and the work"—to strict law; "that they shall do"—to acts beyond the requirements of the law.[59]

In this quotation, the Talmud contrasts the strict law *(din)* to acts that are *lifnim mishurat ha-din* (beyond the requirements of the law). Similarly, the Talmud states:

For Rabbi Yohanan said: Jerusalem was destroyed only because they gave judgements therein in accordance with biblical law! Well, should they rather have followed the law of the Magians? Say, rather because they based their judgements solely upon biblical law and did not act *lifnim mishurat ha-din*—and did not go beyond the requirements of the law.[60]

An interesting application of the *lifnim mishurat ha-din* concept is found in the following story:

Rabbi Yehudah once followed Mar Samuel into a crowded street and he asked him: What if one found here a purse (would he be entitled to keep it)? Mar Samuel answered: It would belong to the finder. What if an Israelite came and indicated an identification mark? Mar Samuel answered: He would have to return it. Thereupon Rabbi Yehudah questioned: But do not the two views contradict each other? Mar Samuel answered: He should go beyond the requirements of the law. Thus, the father of Samuel found some donkeys in the desert, and he returned them to their owner after a year. He went beyond the requirements of the law.[61]

There exists the strict law *(din)* that is obligatory and the concept of *lifnim mishurat ha-din* (going beyond the requirements of the law). Whether the latter is a sort of extra-credit morality or an inner code for those aspiring toward higher spiritual perfection or a moral duty expected of every Jew is not all that clear. Yet, from one talmudic source it would appear that the *lifnim mishurat ha-din* morality is even legally actionable in a court of law. The following incident confirms this principle:

> Some porters negligently broke a barrel of wine belonging to Rabbah son of Rabbi Huna. Thereupon he seized their garments [which were left in his possession in order to guarantee restitution for the damage], and they went to Rav to complain. "Return their garments," he ordered. "Is it the law?" he [Rabbah] inquired. "Even so," he [Rav] rejoined: "That you may walk in the way of good men" (Proverbs 2:20). Their garments having been returned, they observed, "We are poor men, have worked all day, and are in need: are we to get nothing?" "Go and pay them," he ordered. "Is this the law?", he asked. "Even so," was his reply. "And keep the path of the righteous" (Proverbs 2:20).[62]

In connection with this story, Adin Steinsaltz comments that to "a man of his calibre, who can afford the loss and who aspires to do more than is dictated by the inflexible legal code, *mishnat hasidim* (the teaching of the pious) is not only a question of free choice but a duty."[63]

Regarding the *mishnat hasidim* mentioned by Steinsaltz, the following intriguing story is told in the Palestinian Talmud:

> Ulla bar Kosheb was sought for the (Roman) government. He fled, and took refuge at Lud with Rabbi Yehoshua ben Levi. They came and told the inhabitants that the place would be laid waste unless he were given up. Rabbi Yehoshua went and persuaded Ulla that he should let himself be delivered up. Now, Elijah was in the habit of appearing to Rabbi Yehoshua, and he came no more. Then Rabbi Yehoshua fasted many days, and at last Elijah appeared. He (Elijah) said to Rabbi Yehoshua, "Should I reveal myself to informers?" "I did but act according to a teaching," said Rabbi Yehoshua. "Is that a teaching for the pious?" said Elijah.[64]

Ulla bar Kosheb had probably committed a political offense against the ruling power, and he sought refuge in the home of the famous teacher and sage Rabbi Yehoshua ben Levi. Only after government troops were dispatched and after they threatened to destroy the city of Lud if Ulla was not handed over to them did Rabbi Yehoshua persuade his guest to give himself up. Rabbi Yehoshua felt that Ulla's surrender, though it would mean certain death, was completely justified. He based his decision on the text of a talmudic teaching that states, "If a company of Israelites on a journey meet a band of heathens who say, deliver us one of you that we may kill him, otherwise we shall kill you all, they must rather all be killed. However, if they say, deliver us such a one (a named individual), then they may deliver him up."[65]

The above teaching, though legally binding, is not considered a *mishnat hasidim* (a teaching for the pious). The ruling invoked by Rabbi Yehoshua ben Levi was not meant for men excelling in piety. Concerning such situations where this type of double standard exists, David Daube writes, "Where there is a double standard, the idea may be either that the general laws are adequate though the elite must do something extra, or that only the code of the elite is adequate while the general laws constitute a concession to the ordinary man's weakness."[66]

What exactly is the *mishnat hasidim* and the proper course of action to be taken in the situation just described? The Talmud is silent on this matter and leaves it to our imagination. Perhaps Rabbi Yehoshua should have offered himself as a substitute or should have prayed to God.

In another version of this same story, Elijah's reprimand, "Is that a teaching for the pious?" is expanded upon and the prophet goes on to say, "it was needful for this thing to be done by others and not by yourself."[67] Accordingly, Elijah did not object to the actual surrender of Ulla but to the manner in which it was handled. It was not for Rabbi Yehoshua to deal with this matter himself, and others should have been involved as well.

Irrespective of what course of action was to be followed, the point of the story is well taken. The *hasid* (he who aspires to higher spiritual standards) is one who acts inside the line of the law *(lifnim mishurat ha-din)*. This should not be taken to mean that there exists an ethic independent of *halakhah*. This point is clearly stated by Aharon Lichtenstein: "Traditional halakhic Judaism demands of the Jew both adherence to *halakhah* and commitment to an ethical moment that, though different from *halakhah,* is nevertheless of a piece with it and in its own way fully imperative."[68]

CATEGORIES OF MORALITY

Akin to the principles of *lifnim mishurat ha-din* and *mishnat hasidim* are other talmudic categories of morality. One such principle addresses that which is "exempt from human law and culpable according to divine law."[69] Thus, the Talmud speaks of the case where a person hands a flickering coal to an imbecile or a minor. The imbecile or minor fans the flickering coal into a flame, causing a fire that destroys another's property.[70] Though the one who handed over the coal cannot be held legally responsible for the ensuing damages, he is nevertheless morally obligated to compensate for such damages, since he was indirectly involved.

Similarly, the *Mishnah* rules that if a man who wishes to repent says to two others, "I robbed one of you of a *maneh* (an amount of silver), but I do not know which of you I robbed," he must give each a *maneh*.[71] In this case, he is not legally obligated to pay both of them. However, morally, the only way to atone for his crime is to pay both men and thus make sure neither of them suffered a loss because of his act.

Questions of ethics and morality concerning issues of priority and precedence are frequently discussed in the Talmud. Regarding the biblical law requiring one to return a lost article to its owner, the Talmud teaches that "if a man's own lost article and his father's lost article need attention, his own takes precedence."[72] The basis for this ruling is explained by the Talmud in terms of "your own has priority over that of any man,"[73] for no person is obliged to suffer loss as a result of aiding a friend.

This very same logic is applied by Rabbi Akiva in the following hypothetical situation:

> Two men are travelling on a journey (far from civilization), and only one has a pitcher of water. If both drink, they will both die. If one only drinks, he can reach civilization. Ben Patura taught: It is better that both should drink and die, rather than one should behold his companion's death. Until Rabbi Akiva came and taught: "That your brother may live with you" (Leviticus 25:36), your life takes precedence over his life.[74]

AVOT: AN ETHICAL TREATISE

No discussion of talmudic ethics would be complete without mention of the tractate called *Avot. Avot,* usually referred to as "Ethics of the Fathers," is a tractate of the *Mishnah.* Unlike the rest of the *Mishnah,* it contains no legal material but consists exclusively of rabbinic moral maxims and homilies and expounds only values and ideals. The nature of these ethical sayings seems to be based upon reason and human experience. However, careful analysis shows that they are presented in the framework of the chain of tradition and as part of the Oral Law. In fact, the ethical teachings of *Avot* are neither the result of speculative reasoning alone nor of commandments explicitly mentioned in the Bible. In fact, the teachings of *Avot* are ethical principles inferred by the rabbis from biblical texts and narratives. The sages analyzed and expanded upon the specific biblical ethical directives. In so doing, the rabbis have introduced to us a new level of ethics—ethics determined by human experience within the realm of the biblical imperative.[75]

The tractate *Avot* has enjoyed great popularity among the Jewish masses. It has the distinction, unlike any other complete work, of being embodied in the *Siddur* (the *Jewish Prayer Book*). As early as the geonic or posttalmudic era, it became the practice to study a chapter of *Avot* on Saturday afternoons. The prevailing custom among Ashkenazic or European Jewry is to study a chapter from the Sabbath after Passover to the Sabbath before the New Year (Rosh Hashanah). This practice of studying *Avot* in the springtime is most appropriate. One commentator says, "The warm, vital forces of regeneration begin to stir and flow. Man, too, feels powerful instinctual urges rouse within himself. At this time of year it is therefore best to listen to the wisdom of the Sages, to learn how to overcome temptation and passion, develop our will power and control our actions."[76]

The special place *Avot* has in the hearts of the Jewish people is graphically described by the late chief rabbi of Great Britain, Joseph Hertz:

> Sabbath by Sabbath parents studied these wise and edifying maxims with their children, and stressed their moral application; with the result, that the words became part of both Jewish speech and life. The humblest Jewish workman, who had no opportunity for deep Talmudic study, had his *Siddur,* and was usually well versed in the contents of *Avot* reprinted therein. Its influence in moulding the character of the Jew has consequently been as great as it has been beneficient.[77]

The importance and esteem of Avot is further attested to by the fact that the sages advised that he who wishes to be a pious man (a *hasid*) should observe the teachings of *Avot*.[78] For it is through the teachings of *Avot* that one becomes aware of the necessity to carry himself above and beyond the strict letter of the law.

THE WAY OF *HALAKHAH*

The word *halakhah* comes from the Hebrew word *halokh* (to walk). Thus, *halakhah* means the "way in which one walks" or "the path one is to pursue." To be more precise, *halakhah* refers to the whole corpus of Torah law. Unlike the Greeks, to whom law was merely philosophy, and the Romans, to whom law was a science, the sages of the Talmud considered law a religion—a way of life. In fact, the Hebrew word *dat* means both religion and law.

The well-known psychoanalyst and social philosopher Erich Fromm, in discussing the question as to whether Judaism is an ethical rather than a religious system, points to the centrality of *halakhah* in Judaism. *Halakhah,* he writes, demands that

> ... man must act not only according to general principles of justice, truth, and love, but that every act of life be "sanctified," becoming imbued with a religious spirit. "Right action" refers to everything, to the prayer in the morning, to the benediction over food, to the sight of the ocean and of the first flower of the season, to helping the poor, to visiting the sick, to not making a man ashamed in the presence of others.[79]

Though *halakhah* does not openly deal with issues of theology and belief, such concepts nevertheless lie at the core of the *halakhah*. Therefore the study of talmudic thought requires a thorough examination of the *halakhah*. But this is by no means a simple task. First and foremost, one must be completely versed in all areas of talmudic law and jurisprudence. Likewise, a thorough training in the theological and philosophical disciplines is needed. Jacob Neusner writes, "If therefore we want to describe what Judaism teaches, we have to make sense of what Judaism requires the practitioner of Judaism to practice."[80]

THREE PRINCIPLES OF HALAKHIC JUDAISM

The halakhic way of life rests upon three basic principles. First is the recognition that God exists as the sole and absolute good. *Halakhah* is predicated upon *imitatio dei* (the imitation of God). In fact, the term *halakhah* is derived from the biblical phrase "to walk in the ways of God." We imitate God by attempting to follow the good and right way of living. The way of *halakhah* leads man to a closeness with God, the attainment of the very goal for which man was created. Thus, living according to halakhah affords one not only the opportunity of happiness and good life but also the unfolding within man of the divine image.

The second premise of *halakhah* is that the Torah, both Written and Oral, is part of a divinely ordained system. As such it constitutes the ultimate truth. David S. Shapiro, in his penetrating essay entitled, "The Ideological Foundations of the Halakhah," says, "The Halakhah is a Revelation which emanates from the One Shepherd of Israel. We must endeavor to find the Revealer in the Revelation in all aspects, ramifications, and divergencies."[81]

Third is the halakhic premise that is based on the belief that man must be totally committed to the service of God. In the *midrash* we read, "Rabbi Elazar of Modi'in said: If a man says, I accept all the Torah with one exception . . . he has despised the word of the Lord. . . ."[82] It is man's free submission to God's will that enables him to elevate himself above the animal and subhuman. A frequent theme in the Talmud is that he who is bound by the *mitzvot* has attained the true status of humanity.

MAN IN HIS MUNDANE ENVIRONMENT

A closer look at the halakhic scheme shows it is all-embracing. *Halakhah* deals with man as a human being in his mundane environment. The dedication and commitment demanded by the halakhic way of life is not confined to the temple or synagogue. It guides man in every single move he makes. In fact, *halakhah* is even concerned with man's fate after death. The belief in reward and punishment in this life as well as after death is a fundamental halakhic doctrine. Shapiro explains, "It is a presupposition of the *Halakhah* that, by fulfilling his responsibilities in accordance with the Divine Will, man's personality is elevated beyond its physical substratum and acquires the capacity to transcend death."[83]

Unlike other religious doctrines, Judaism, as expressed by the *halakhah,* does not shun worldly pleasures. Asceticism and withdrawal are alien to the halakhic way. It is this very outlook that prompted the famous teacher Rav to say, "A man will have to give account on the judgement day of every good permissible thing which he might have enjoyed and did not."[84] Thus, *halakhah* serves as a master plan for human existence within the realities of the world.

Diet and Table Etiquette

For a closer examination of this concept let us look at some of the *halakhot* dealing with diet and table etiquette. Eating is an instinctive biological function man shares with the animals. But *halakhah* demands of man that he raise himself above the animal level. Thus, Jewish law requires that one go through a complete ritual before and after partaking of any food. The ritual includes washing of the hands, reciting various blessings, and the saying of grace after the meal. The food itself must be fit and proper; the slaughtering of animals and the preparation of the food must carefully conform to halakhic requirements. By following the way of *halakhah,* man submits to a life of responsibility. It is through the acceptance of the *mitzvot* (the commandments) as norms of behavior that man attains the level and status of a human being.

The Talmud teaches that although man cannot fathom the reasons for all the commandments, the rationale for many of them is not that God needs their fulfillment but rather that they are an exercise in the attainment of human perfection. The *midrash* states:

> What does God care whether a man kills an animal in the proper way and eats it, or whether he strangles the animal and eats it? Will the one benefit Him, or the other injure Him? Or what does God care whether a man eats unclean animals or clean animals? So you learn that the commandments were given only to purify God's creatures, as it says "God's word is purified, it is a protection to those who trust in Him" (2 Samuel 22:31).[85]

What the rabbis of the *midrash* are saying is that man's observance of the divine imperatives does not profit God in any way. The Torah was given to man for the benefit of humankind. Rabbi Joseph B. Soloveitchik, the preeminent talmudic scholar, writes:

> The Halacha demands that man purge himself in order to achieve his full worth. Isaiah, describing the future redemption of Israel, speaks of purgation as an indispensable condition of redemption: "I shall cleanse thy dross as with soap" (Isaiah 1:25). Similarly, our Rabbis have stated repeatedly that the purpose which Torah and Mitzvot pursue is that of purification of the human being. In other words, catharsis is a *sine qua non* for a meaningful existence which Halacha approves.[86]

This halakhic catharsis of which Rabbi Soloveitchik speaks applies to different aspects of man's life—to the realm of man's physical pleasures, his emotional world, his intellectual and moral-religious world, as well as to his relationship with God. Another important dimension of the *halakhah,* as perceived by the rabbis of the Talmud, is its clear indication that the ideal life is not to be sought in the transcendental world but may be found right here on earth. This idea is succinctly stated by the sages in tractate *Avot:* "Better is one hour of repentance and good deeds in this world than a whole life in the world to come."[87]

Through *halakhah,* man can reach his highest perfection by bringing the kingdom of heaven down to earth. That the stage of life, according to *halakhah,* is the here and now manifests itself in many ways. Contrary to other religious systems in which death is idealized as the threshold to the beyond, *halakhah* holds that with the exception of the three cardinal sins—idolatry, immorality, and murder—the preservation of human life takes precedence over all divine commandments.[88] Even the laws of the Sabbath are to be set aside in order to save a human life. The *midrash* relates:

> That once it happened that letters from the Roman government, containing evil tidings for the Jews, reached the elders of Sepphoris. They came and asked Rabbi Elazar ben Perata what to do. It was on the Sabbath, and they said, "Should we flee?" Whereupon it was expounded: Danger to life annuls the Sabbath, for man is to live by doing God's commandments and not to die by them.[89]

A basic objective of the *halakhah* is the sanctification of the mundane. *Kedushah* (sanctification) is multifaceted. Prior to the performance of a particular *mitzvah* (commandment), *halakhah* requires that a specific benediction be recited. This emphasizes that one acquires sanctity by means of fulfilling the commandments. Furthermore, through *halakhah,* God endowed man with the potential of transforming time and space into domains of holiness. For example, the dates of the holy festivals are determined by means of man's calculations of the calendar. So too is a Torah scroll holy, provided the scribe intended to sanctify it.

THE SABBATH

The Bible frequently enjoins the Israelites to rest on the Sabbath. In the positive sense, one is to "remember the Sabbath to keep it holy,"[90] and negatively speaking, we are enjoined, "Do not do anything that constitutes work."[91] However, the Written Law does not specifically define *work*. It is to the Oral Law that we must turn to gain further insight into the nature of the Sabbath.

Based on the fact that the Bible states the Sabbath was not to be desecrated even for the building of the Sanctuary, the Talmud concludes that the definition of *work* is any activity associated with the building of the Sanctuary. According to Oral Tradition, there are thirty-nine categories of work prohibited on the Sabbath. Included among the thirty-nine are carrying, cooking, lighting fires, all agricultural activities, writing, building, making cloth, sewing, making leather, laundering, and assembling articles.[92] Upon careful examination of these prohibited activities, one notes that they are representative of various types of human creativity, irrespective of their strenuous nature.

Going further, the rabbis of the Talmud stated, *melekhet mahshevet aserah Torah* ("the Torah forbids as work the realization of an intelligent purpose by practical skill").[93] Thus, the *halakhah* teaches that an act of pure destruction, however strenuous, is not construed as a biblical violation of work on the Sabbath, inasmuch as it lacks any constructive purpose. On the other hand, if one were to destroy a building with the constructive purpose of clearing the site for rebuilding, such an act would be considered a *melakhah* (a prohibited activity).

Likewise, the laws concerning carrying need not necessarily involve physical labor. Even the mere carrying of a handkerchief on the Sabbath in a public domain is prohibited. Carrying from one domain to another is characteristic of man's pursuit and attainment of purpose in the realm of human society. Carrying emphasizes man's activity in the social realm, the "circulating of material goods between house and house, through street and thoroughfare; not for trade only, but also for the personal and social ends of everyday life."[94]

By refraining from carrying on the Sabbath, we acknowledge God as our Master in the sphere of human society as well as the natural environment. This sorely misunderstood concept of talmudic law is eloquently explained by Erich Fromm:

> The point is that not the effort of carrying a load is forbidden, but the transfer of any object from one privately owned piece of land to another, because such transfer constituted, originally a transfer of property. On the Sabbath one lives as if one has nothing, pursuing no aim except being. That is, expressing one's essential powers: praying, studying, eating, drinking, singing, making love.[95]

In the talmudic scheme, the *halakhah* always reflects the purpose of the particular biblical commandment—the purpose being implemented by means of *halakhah*.

Concerning the Sabbath, the Bible states that its observance testifies that God is the Supreme Creator of the world. For six days of the week, man engages in a constant struggle for mastery over God's creation, often forgetting the source of his very power of conquest. It is to this issue that the halakhic Sabbath regulations address themselves. By observing the Sabbath rest, according to *halakhah,* one is reminded of his dependence upon God as the true Master of the Universe.

Unlike the ancient Babylonian *Shapatu,* which was a day of fear and sadness, the talmudic sages proclaimed the Sabbath a day of beauty and light. Rabbi Hiyya ben Abba said, "The Sabbath was given for enjoyment."[96] The various halakhic regulations of the Sabbath were not intended to create a day of hardship, sorrow, and anxiety. On the Sabbath, teaches the Talmud, he who keeps the day in strict accordance with the

Torah is blessed with an "additional soul"[97] that brings him the highest form of spiritual joy. Rabbi Hanina said it was only with reluctance that the rabbis allowed mourners to be comforted or the sick to be visited on the Sabbath.[98] Unlike the modern Sunday, which "is a day of fun, consumption, and running from oneself,"[99] the halakhic Sabbath stresses a day of peace, harmony, and attainment of spiritual perfection.

This special character of the Sabbath was expressed in a short prayer recited by Rabbi Zadok on Sabbath nights:

> Through the love which You, O Lord our God, lovest Your people Israel, and the mercy which You have shown to the children of Your covenant, You have given unto us in love this great and holy seventh day.[100]

ROLE OF THE INTELLECT

Basic to the halakhic scheme is the role of the intellect, the academic study of the Torah. The Talmud relates that Rabbi Tarfon and the elders were once reclining in the upper story of Nithza's house, in Lydda, when they were confronted with the question, which is greater, study or practice? Rabbi Tarfon answered, "Practice is greater." Rabbi Akiva claimed that "study is greater, for it leads to practice." Then they all responded by saying, "Study is greater, for it leads to action."[101] Study is a necessary prerequisite for the leading of a life according to *halakhah*. As the great Hillel used to say, "An empty-headed man cannot be sin fearing, nor can an ignorant person be pious."[102] Study was of such importance that it even took precedence over doing. It is told that Raba, upon noticing how Rav Hamnuna prolonged his prayer, declared, "Such men neglect the eternal life, and busy themselves with the life of the hour."[103] Raba maintained that there is a set time for prayer and a set time for study of the Torah. Similarly, we are told that Rabbi Jeremiah sat before Rav Ze'era, and they were busy in the study of a legal question; the time for saying the evening prayer passed. While Rabbi Jeremiah hastened to say it, Rav Ze'era chastised him by quoting, "He who turns his ear from hearing the Torah, his very prayer is an abomination."[104]

TORAH LISHMAH

However, in addition to study serving as a means to an end, it is an end in itself. *Torah lishmah* (the study of Torah for its own sake) is in many respects akin to worship. Through the study of Torah, one is brought closer to God. It is as if the divine revelation is set open before him.

Rabbi Meir taught, "Whoever occupies himself with the study of Torah for its own sake merits many things, and not only that, but the entire world is worthwhile because of him."[105] According to Rabbi Meir, he who has studied *Torah lishmah* has justified the very creation and existence of the world. According to the Talmud, God created the world on condition that the people of Israel accept the Torah. Commenting on the verse, "Were it not for my covenant, day and night, I would not have appointed the ordinances of heaven and earth,"[106] the Talmud explains that God made the existence of the world contingent on the continuous study of the Torah by Israel.[107] It is this idea that the great teacher Rav spoke of when he said that he who studies Torah for its own sake is a builder of the Almighty's palace of the heavenly realm and of His terrestrial palace here below.[108]

David S. Shapiro sums up the significance of *Torah lishmah* as follows:

Study of the Torah as the supreme obligation of the Jew is not divorced from *Imitatio Dei,* even when this study is not pragmatically oriented, for study was never meant to be a mere intellectual exercise, but rather a means for the ennoblement of the spirit of man. "Whosoever is engaged in study of the Torah for its own sake will achieve many things. He will become a lover of God and a lover of His creatures. He will bring joy to God and joy to His creatures." Even engrossment in the purely theoretical aspects of the Torah has its effect upon one who studies for its own sake. This study is the equivalent of performance where the sacred act cannot be actualized. The moral goal toward which the commandment is directed is implemented in the orientation of the heart toward that goal.[109]

The halakhic way leads to the perfection and purification of mankind, with the ultimate goal of achieving peace in the world.[110]

11
THE TALMUD TODAY: ITS IMPACT AND INFLUENCE

T hroughout the centuries, the Jew studied the Talmud and shaped his life according to its teachings. However, *The Essence of Talmudic Law and Thought* remains incomplete without mention of the impact of the Talmud on East European Jewry of the pre-Holocaust period.

TALMUD: A LIVING TRADITION

The Jew, whether living in the *shtetl* (rural village) or in the big city, was affected in one way or another by the Talmud. To the East European Jew, the study of the Talmud and its related rabbinic writings was of the highest priority. "The Torah is the highest good," and "My little child, close your eyes; if God will, you'll be a rabbi."[1] These were familiar words of lullabies sung by Jewish mothers. When the young child was taken for the first time to *heder* (religious school), he was wrapped in a *talit* (a prayer shawl) like a Torah scroll. It was the aspiration of all parents that their children grow up to be talmudic scholars. Women sacrificed their time and energies to enable their husbands to devote themselves to Torah study. In almost every home, the volumes of the Talmud and other rabbinic writings were proudly displayed.

Abraham Joshua Heschel, in his moving account of the inner spirit of East European Jewish life, writes:

> In almost every Jewish home in Eastern Europe, even in the humblest and the poorest, stood a bookcase full of volumes; proud and stately folio tomes together with shy, small-sized books. Books were neither an asylum for the frustrated nor a means for occasional edification. They were furnaces of living strength, time-proof receptacles for the eternally valid coins of spirit.[2]

People in all walks of life—student and scholar, rich and poor, sophisticate and simpleton—all spent time in the *bet ha-midrash* (the study house) studying, or better yet, "learning" Torah and Talmud. A Christian scholar, while visiting Warsaw during the early part of this century, noticed

> a great many coaches on a parking place but with no drivers in sight. In my own country, I would have known where to look for them. A young Jewish boy showed me the way: In a courtyard, on the second floor, was the *shtibl* (the small synagogue) of the Jewish drivers. It consisted of two rooms: one filled with Talmud-volumes, the other a room for prayer. All the drivers were engaged in fervent study and religious discussion. . . . It was then that I found out and became convinced that all professions, the bakers, the butchers, the shoemakers, etc., have their own *shtibl* in the Jewish district; and every free moment which can be taken off from their work is given to the study of the Torah. And when they get together in intimate groups, one urges the other: "Sog mir a shtickl Torah—Tell me a little Torah."[3]

The learning of the East European Jew was virtually *Torah lishmah*. Those parts of the Talmud that were totally irrelevant to the daily life of the European Jew were studied with the same zeal and enthusiasm as those having a direct bearing on his daily life. The study of the Talmud was a spiritual adventure. Standing over his *shtender* (reading stand), the Jew would chant to the tune of a *nigun* (melody) the dialectical discussions of the *Gemara*.

This unique spiritual encounter with the Talmud is demonstrated by the following tale:

> Rabbi Zusya of Hanipol once started to study a volume of the Talmud. A day later, his disciples noticed that he was still dwelling on the first page. They assumed that he must have encountered a difficult passage and was trying to solve it. But when a number of days passed and he was still immersed in the first page, they were astonished, but did not dare to query the master. Finally one of them gathered courage and asked him why he did not proceed to the next page. And Rabbi Zusya answered: "I feel so good here, why should I go elsewhere?"[4]

Institutions of higher learning devoted to the study of Talmud dotted the map of Eastern Europe. *Yeshivot* (academies of learning) have their origin in talmudic times, and throughout the medieval period prominent academies of Jewish learning existed in France, Germany, Spain, and North Africa.

THE TALMUDICAL ACADEMY: THE *YESHIVAH*

The modern version of the *yeshivah* was organized and founded by Rabbi Hayyim of Volozin in 1802. Rabbi Hayyim was a disciple of the famed Rabbi Elijah, the Gaon of Vilna, and fashioned his *yeshivah* in accordance with the principles and methods of his great teacher. The *yeshivah* was located in the town of Volozin, a small distance from Vilna, in Lithuania.

It was organized as an independent institution not affiliated with or reliant on the local Jewish community. Students attending the school devoted all their time to the intensive study of the Talmud and its related writings. It was not a professional school, and it did not train or ordain rabbis.

The daily routine of study in the Volozin *Yeshivah* is described by William B. Helmreich:

> Inspired by his leadership, challenged by the high standards he set, students from all parts of the world vied for acceptance at Reb Chaim's yeshiva, known as the Etz Chaim Yeshiva. Once they were there, the requirements were informal. No formal examinations were given; instead, the heads of the yeshiva would engage the students in conversations about their work. The young men, or *bochorim,* studied in pairs or *chavrusas,* sometimes engaging older students to help them. Since most *bochorim* depended on the yeshiva for income, they had to make do with "bread and tea for breakfast and supper, bread and some warm dish for luncheon, and meat once a week—on the Sabbath."[5]

When Rabbi Naftali Zvi Yehudah Berlin[6] assumed the position of *rosh yeshivah* (dean) in 1854, a more rigorous program of study was introduced. The *havruta* method was retained. However, daily classes and regular examinations were now introduced. The *yeshivah* of Volozin was to become the model for all subsequent Lithuanian *yeshivot.*

Pre-Holocaust East European Jewry could boast of many outstanding *yeshivot,* such as Mir, Telshe, Slabodka, Radin, and Kamanetz. Young gifted men from far and wide were attracted to these citadels of talmudic learning. The curricula of all these schools were similar—in practice only eight tractates of the Babylonian Talmud were studied on a cyclical basis. They were generally chosen from the Orders of *Nezikin* and *Nashim,* dealing with aspects of civil and family law. The method of study was textual, and it was based on the analytical and synthetic approaches. Some of the greatest Jewish minds of pre-Holocaust Europe attended the *yeshivot* of Lithuania. Many of their alumni included leading writers, poets, politicians, and scientists, as well as prominent rabbis and Jewish scholars.[7]

This rich and productive period of Jewish learning came to an abrupt end in Hitler's war against the Jews. Thousands of students and rabbis died. A small remnant successfully escaped via Vilna, eventually making their way to Israel and the United States. Eventually, many of these famous *yeshivot* were transplanted to American and Israeli soil.

DAF YOMI

In recent times, there has been an upsurge of interest in the study of the Talmud. Not only are thousands of college-age young men attending the many talmudical academies in America and Israel, but laymen of all walks of life are devoting time to the study of Talmud. In 1924, a leading Polish rabbi, Meir Shapiro, proposed that every Jew undertake to study one identical page of the Babylonian Talmud each day. According to the plan, called *Daf Yomi* (Daily Page), the entire Babylonian Talmud is completed every seven years, followed with a communal *Siyum* (Completion) celebration. Although the *Daf Yomi* program was inaugurated some sixty years ago, it is only in recent times that we have witnessed renewed interest in it. In fact, the most recent innovation, "Dial a Daf," enables one to study the "Daily Page" by telephone. Similar projects, such as *Mishnah Yomit* (a daily study of the *Mishnah*) and *Daf ha-Shavuah* (wherein a page of the Talmud is studied in the course of one week) have been established. Some of these programs are broadcast on radio on a regular basis and are heard by thousands of listeners.

TALMUD AND JEWISH SURVIVAL

Although the academic pursuit of the Talmud is of vital importance, the impact of talmudic thought on Jewish life goes beyond that. Of all the ancient religions and cultures, only Judaism was able to withstand the cultural, economic, and political erosion of the times. Despite the loss of the Jewish homeland and the destruction of the Holy Temple in Jerusalem nearly two thousand years ago, Judaism has persisted through centuries of persecution and wandering. To pinpoint the source of this inner strength and drive is no simple task. However, it would be no exaggeration to say that the Talmud has been a significant factor in this marvelous miracle of Jewish existence.

Even more than the Bible, the Talmud has been the very source and pillar of Jewish culture. All facets of Jewish learning and culture, in one way or another, have been influenced by the Talmud and the teachings of the sages. Of course, Jewish religious observance and dogma are directly based upon the traditions of the Oral Law as embodied in the Talmud. The great Jewish codes of law, such as Maimonides' *Mishneh Torah* and Rabbi Joseph Karo's *Shulhan Arukh,* which to this very day serve as guides for the observant Jew, are merely restatements of talmudic law as interpreted by the rabbinic scholars of medieval times.[8]

In a way, the Talmud has never been completed. In modern times, new and challenging issues and questions pertaining to Jewish law are being analyzed and decided on within the framework and methodology of talmudic thought and jurisprudence. Although ancient halakhic principles are as applicable today as they were in the past, leading talmudists of our day are preoccupied with questions of contemporary relevance. Among them are questions ranging from women's rights,[9] euthanasia,[10] and capital punishment[11] to issues concerning abortion,[12] extraterrestrial life,[13] and genetic engineering.[14] There is no question or issue, no matter how "modern," that cannot be resolved according to talmudic methodology and halakhic concepts. Thus, the literature of the Talmud gave birth to a vast network of *Responsa* literature. These are collections of responses to questions addressed to talmudic scholars.

Likewise, other branches of Jewish learning have been influenced by the Talmud. Biblical exegesis (the interpretation of the Bible) cannot be properly pursued without recourse to the writings of the *midrash* and Talmud. The basic rudiments of Jewish philosophy go back to the *aggadah* and theology of the sages of the Talmud. Countless poets, both medieval and modern, were directly inspired by the warmth and profundity of talmudic lore and legend. For a true appreciation of the fiction of authors such as Agnon, Potok, and Singer, an understanding of talmudic tradition is indispensable.

The importance of the Talmud for the survival of the Jewish people cannot be underestimated. The sociohistorical implications of the Talmud have been underscored by Adin Steinsaltz:

It is reasonably certain that no Jewish community could survive for long without the ability to study Talmud. Some communities did not produce scholars from their midst because of material poverty, lack of suitable candidates (as a result of the decrees of the authorities), or indifference. Whatever the reason, however, the fact is they did not survive for long. In the course of Jewish history, various ethnic communities have tried to maintain their Judaism, sometimes even on a strictly traditional basis, without Talmudic scholarship. The same process occurred in all of them; the components of their Judaism were weakened and began to disintegrate, the deeper significance of issues was no longer fully understood, and inappropriate interpretations were evolved, so that despite sincere efforts to maintain traditions, such communities lost their vitality and died out. Sometimes the process was protracted, with tradition gradually becoming more and more a matter of outward show for lack of sages capable of endowing it with a new life, and assimilation inevitably followed. Sometimes the catastrophe came swiftly; strong external pressures were exerted on the Jews, and many were unable to withstand them and abandoned their Judaism.[15]

An example of this phenomenon was the state of affairs pertaining to the Jews living in the western part of the Roman Empire between the fourth and eighth centuries. During these centuries, two powerful forces shook the Roman Empire. First, there were the repeated invasions of the barbarians, sweeping across the western Roman Empire. In the course of their violent and ravaging attacks, towns and cities were looted and destroyed. A large segment of the Jewish population, which was made up mainly of town dwellers, was destroyed. Second was the powerful effort of the Christian church to convert all non-Gentiles in the Roman Empire. The pressure on the Jews to convert to Christianity was at times unbearable. During the seventh century and the first half of the eighth century, it was almost impossible to live openly as a Jew in Germany, France, and northern Italy. By the end of the eighth century, only a mere handful of Jews—about five to ten thousand—survived as Jews in those three countries.

It has been shown that the survival of these people as Jews was largely due to their dedication and loyalty to the talmudic way of life and emphasis on *halakhah*. Irving A. Agus, a historian of the medieval period, explains:

> The intelligent members of the group learned very quickly how to hide and how to save their families and their wealth quite effectively. . . . To survive the critical period following an invasion, great intelligence and unusual adaptability were required. . . .
>
> To resist this mounting pressure of the Church for more than four centuries, required tremendous strength of character. It required unusual stamina, great heroism, and unimaginably strong devotion to Judaism—the type of devotion that comes only from a life-long dedication to the study of the Oral Law.[16]

The devotion of the Jew to the study of Torah and Talmud as a source of his very survival is most dramatically encountered during the period of the Holocaust. In the Dautmorgan camp in southern Germany, a group of *yeshivah* students would get together nightly to study the *Mishnah*. Exhausted and close to starvation, they would gather around a thin, white-faced lad from Navorodok, who would recite out loud the text of the *Mishnah* from memory. In Garelitz, Yankel Pick, a young inmate at the Gross-Rosen concentration camp, would study Talmud during the daily march from the block to the machine factory where he worked. Yankel would arrange for other inmates of Block Six to march alongside him each morning. Together, to the *nigun* (melody) of the Talmud study, they marched to the factory.[17]

Hillel Seidman, the Yiddish journalist, writing in his diary of the Warsaw ghetto, recalls how rabbis, scholars, and layman alike gathered in Schultz's cobbler's shop to study Talmud:

> Gemarot and biblical texts are quoted . . . and who cares now about the SS men, about the Volksdeutsch supervisor, or about hunger, misery, persecutions, and fear of death! Now they are soaring in higher regions, they are not in the "shop" at 46 Nowolipie Street where they are sitting, but in lofty halls. . . .[18]

The importance of the Talmud as a source of Jewish survival is most poignantly set forth by Hayyim Nahman Bialik, the renowned poet of modern times, in the poem entitled, "And Should You Wish to Know":

> And should you wish to find the Spring from which your banished people drew,
> Midst fear of death and fear of life, their comfort, courage, patience, trust, an iron will to bear their yoke,
> To live bespattered and despised, and suffer without end?

And should you wish to see the Fort wherein your fathers refuge
    sought,
And all their sacred treasures hid,
The refuge that has still preserved your nation's soul intact and
    pure,
And when despised, and scorned, and scoffed, Their faith they did
    not shame?

Then enter the House of God, the House of Study, old and gray,
Throughout the sultry summer days,
Throughout the gloomy winter nights,
At morning, midday, or at eve;
Per chance there is a remnant yet,
Per chance your eye may still behold

In some dark corner, hid from view, a cast off shadow of the past,
The profile of some pallid face, upon an ancient folio bent,
Who seeks to drown unspoken woes in the Talmudic boundless
    waves;
And then your heart shall guess the truth, that you have touched
    the sacred ground of your nation's House of Life
And that your eyes gaze upon the treasures of your nation's soul.

And know that this is but a spark, that by a miracle escaped
Of that bright light, that sacred flame
Your forbears kindled long ago
On altars high and pure.[19]

SEARCHING FOR THE TRUTH

The analytical and dialectical way of the Talmud has also left
its mark upon the Jewish people. The rabbis of the Talmud
emphasized the critical, analytical, and theoretical aspects of
human thought. The talmudic format of study is more or less
that of question and answer. Every premise and idea is thor-

oughly investigated and questioned. "No individual can study Talmud," states Adin Steinsaltz, "without being or becoming an eternal skeptic."[20]

This talmudic "skepticism," this searching for the truth, has created an element of self-criticism characteristic of the Jewish people throughout the ages. The sages of the Talmud were religious men committed to conviction and concepts not always amenable to logic. Yet, at the same time, they were men of reason and logic. Within the pages of the Talmud there is a phenomenal blend of faith and reason, belief and skepticism. This remarkable synthesis has remained central to Jewish life. Groping, questioning, and searching, together with an awareness that beyond all of it lies "a reality to which one must adhere"[21]—this has become the hallmark of Jewish existence.

In Jewish tradition, when a tractate of the Talmud is completed, it is customary to recite a short prayer called *Hadran Alakh* ("We Shall Return to Thee"). There is no end to or completion of the study of the Talmud; one never says good-bye. Like the French *au revoir* and the Hebrew *le-hitraot,* the student of the Talmud never permanently leaves the *Gemara;* he will always return to it. The eminent talmudist Rabbi Joseph B. Soloveitchik eloquently explains that "it is just like when a mother leaves her child and says 'I'll be back.' She does not say this merely to encourage the infant. She expresses a basic truth. A mother leaves only to return; otherwise she would not leave."[22]

For all eternity, the Talmud will be loved like the child of that mother.

APPENDIX

CHRONOLOGY

586 B.C.E.	The destruction of the First Temple.
537 B.C.E.	Cyrus's edict and the return to Zion.
457–444 B.C.E.	The coming of Ezra and Nehemiah to Judea.
332 B.C.E.	Alexander the Great conquers the Persian Empire.
301 B.C.E.	Ptolemy I conquers *Eretz Yisrael*.
260 B.C.E.	The beginning of the period of the *Zugot*.
200–100 B.C.E.	The establishment of the Hasmonean dynasty.
63 B.C.E.	Pompey conquers Jerusalem.
31 B.C.E.	Hillel appointed the head of the Sanhedrin.
37–34 B.C.E.	Herod.
6–41 C.E.	Judea, Samaria, and Idumeia formed into a Roman province.
c. 38–100	Josephus.
70	The destruction of the Second Temple.

c. 80	Death of Rabbi Yohanan ben Zakkai.
135	Execution of Rabbi Akiva.
c. 135–220	Rabbi Judah the Prince.
c. 200	The redaction of the *Mishnah.*
c. 200–500	The period of the *amoraim.*
219	Arrival of Rav in Babylonia.
c. 350	Jerusalem Talmud completed.
c. 500–700	Saboraic period.
700–1100	The era of the *geonim.*
c. 1027	Death of Rabbi Husiel.
1028	Death of Rabbenu Gershom.
1040–1105	Rabbi Shlomo Yitzhaki (Rashi).
c. 1055	The death of Rabbi Hananel.
1062	The *Arukh* of Rabbi Nathan of Rome is completed.
1135–1204	Maimonides.
1194–1270	Rabbi Moses ben Nahman (Nahmanides).
1235–1310	Rabbi Shlomo ben Aderet (Rashbah).
1242	Burning of the Talmud in Paris.
1249	Birth of Rabbi Menahem Ha-Meiri.
1475	Beginning of Hebrew printing.
1510–1520	Reuchlin-Pfefferkorn controversy.
1510–1574	Rabbi Solomon Luria.
1520–1523	First complete edition of the Babylonian Talmud printed.
1523–1524	First printing of the Jerusalem Talmud.
1529	The death of Rabbi Jacob Pollack.
1564	Rabbi Joseph Karo's *Shulhan Arukh* published.
1612–1621	Commentary of Rabbi Samuel Edels (Maharsha) published.
1615	The death of Rabbi Meir of Lublin.
1720–1797	Rabbi Elijah, the Gaon of Vilna.
1761–1837	Rabbi Akiva Eger.
1802	The establishment of the Volozin *Yeshivah.*

1831	The death of Rabbi Aryeh Leb Ha-Kohen.
1832	The death of Rabbi Jacob of Lisa.
1853–1918	Rabbi Hayyim Soloveitchik.
1854	Rabbi Naftali Zvi Yehudah Berlin becomes head of the Volozin *Yeshivah*.
1860–1940	Rabbi Shimon Shkop.
1896	The Cairo *Genizah* discovered.

NOTES

INTRODUCTION

1. Though the *Mishnah* consists of 63 tractates, only 37 contain *Gemara*.

2. Adin Steinsaltz, *The Essential Talmud* (New York: Bantam Books, 1976), p. 4.

3. Ibid.

4. Ibid. See also R. Yosef ibn Megas, *Responsa,* no. 114 (Jerusalem: Chaim Gittler, 1959), p. 17a; *Encyclopedia Talmudit,* ed. Shlomo Yosef Zevin, vol. 9 (Jerusalem: World Mizrachi Organization, 1959), pp. 337–338.

5. Solomon Schechter, *Studies in Judaism* (Philadelphia: Jewish Publication Society, 1924), pp. 144–145.

CHAPTER 1

1. The term *sofrim* has two meanings. According to Ezra 7:6, it is derived from the root *sefer* (book or scroll) and refers to both those engaged in the writing or copying of the Torah and the interpreters

or teachers of the law. Another view (*Kiddushin* 30a) maintains that the name *sofrim* comes from the Hebrew *safar* (to count) "because they used to count all the letters of the Torah" in order to safeguard the accuracy of the text.

2. See Alexander Guttmann, *Rabbinic Judaism in the Making* (Detroit: Wayne State University Press, 1970), pp. 7–9.

3. *Avot* 1:1. See Nathan Drazin, *History of Jewish Education from 515 B.C.E. to 220 C.E.* (Baltimore: Johns Hopkins, 1940), pp. 38–43.

4. Cf. Sherira b. Hanina, *Iggeret R. Sherira Gaon,* ed. B. M. Lewin (Jerusalem: Mekor, 1971), p. 39; J. N. Epstein, *Introduction to Tannaitic Literature* (Jerusalem: Magnes–Dvir, 1957), pp. 501–505.

5. *Berakhot* 33a; *Megillah* 17b–18a.

6. *Bava Batra* 15a.

7. See Shlomo Rotenberg, *Toldot Am Olam,* vol. 1 (Jerusalem: Keren Eliezer, 1967), pp. 380–381; Solomon Zeitlin, "An Historical Study of the Canonization of the Hebrew Scriptures," in *The Canon and Masorah of the Hebrew Bible,* ed. Sid Z. Leiman (New York: Ktav, 1974), pp. 164–199.

8. Rotenberg, *Toldot Am Olam,* p. 381.

9. *Mishnah Hagigah* 2:2; *Avot* 1:4–12. Cf. Sidney B. Hoenig, *The Great Sanhedrin* (Philadelphia: Dropsie University Press, 1953), pp. 37–52.

10. Josephus, *Antiquities of the Jews,* Book 13, 5:9, p. 274.

11. J. Gutkowski, *The Era of the Second Temple* (New York: Shengold, 1974), p. 211, n. 2.

12. For a complete description of this sect, see Josephus, *Wars of the Jews,* Book 2, 8:1–13, pp. 476–478.

13. See A. Dupont–Sommer, *The Essene Writings From Qumran* (Oxford: Oxford University, 1961). Yigael Yadin, *The Message of the Scrolls* (New York: Simon and Schuster, 1957), pp. 160–189. There are scholars who maintain that the scrolls are of a later dating. See Sidney B. Hoenig, "Pre-Karaism and the Sectarian (Qumran) Scrolls," in *Joshua Finkel Festschrift* (New York: Yeshiva University Press, 1973), pp. 71–94; "Qumran Fantasies," *The Jewish Quarterly Review,* 63:4(1973):247–268.

14. Gutkowski, *Era of the Second Temple,* pp. 207–211.

15. *Yerushalmi Ketubbot* 8:11; *Bava Batra* 21a.

16. *Yerushalmi Ketubbot* 8:11.

17. Josephus, *Antiquities,* Book 13, 10:6, p. 281.

18. *Avot de-Rabbi Natan* ed. Solomon Schechter (New York: Feldheim, 1967), chap. 4.

19. See chapter 3.

20. See Michael Avi-Yonah, *The Jews of Palestine* (New York: Schocken, 1976), pp. 185–207.

21. 2 Kings 24.

22. 2 Kings 25; Jeremiah 52.

23. Ezra 1.

24. Josephus, *Antiquities,* Book 11, 1:3, p. 228.

25. Prior to Parthian rule, Babylonia fell to Alexander the Great. Upon Alexander's death in 323 B.C.E., Babylonia became the possession of Seleucus Nicator. In about 140 B.C.E. it was captured by the Parthians.

26. Concerning the origin and earliest possible dating of the Exilarchate, see *Seder Olam Zuta* in *Medieval Jewish Chronicles and Chronological Notes,* ed. A. Neubauer, vol. 2 (Oxford: Clarendon Press, 1895), p. 74; Jacob Neusner, *There We Sat Down* (Nashville: Abingdon Press, 1972), pp. 46–51.

27. See *Gittin* 14a–b.

28. Neusner, *There We Sat Down,* p. 30.

29. See *Tosafot, Gittin* 6a, s.v. *me-hi;* Isaac Halevi, *Dorot ha-Rishonim,* vols. 2, 4 (Jerusalem: Mekor, 1966), pp. 206–208, 672–704.

30. *Pesahim* 3b; *Sanhedrin* 32b.

31. *Mishnah Yevamot* 16:7.

32. *Midrash Kohelet Rabbati* 1:25; *Yerushalmi Sanhedrin* 1:2; *Berakhot* 63a.

33. See *Sanhedrin* 13b; Halevi, *Dorot ha-Rishonim,* 4:678.

34. Cf. Samuel K. Mirsky, "The Formation of the Mishnah and the Babylonian Talmud," in *Tractate Endings of the Mishnah and the Babylonian Talmud* (New York: Young Israel Synagogue of Boro Park, 1961), pp. 39–47.

35. Ibid., p. 39.

36. *Berakhot* 35a.

37. Sherira b. Hanina, *Iggeret R. Sherira Gaon,* pp. 69–70. For a

good overview of the saboraic period, see Jacob E. Ephrathi's *The Sevoraic Period and its Literature* (Petah Tikvah: Agudath Bnai Asher, 1973).

CHAPTER 2

1. As to whether the terms *Torah she-Bekhtav* and *Torah she-Ba'al Peh* are identical to the Roman *jus scriptum* and *jus non-scriptum,* see Menahem Elon, *Jewish Law,* vol. 1 (Jerusalem: Magnes, 1973), p. 181.

2. *Berakhot* 5a; *Yerushalmi Peah* 2:4.

3. Samson Raphael Hirsch trans., *The Pentateuch,* vol. 2 (Gateshead: Judaica Press, 1973), pp. 288–289.

4. Exodus 20:5.

5. Deuteronomy 17:8–11.

6. Moses Maimonides, *Introduction to the Commentary on the Mishnah,* pp. 81–98. Two important studies dealing with Maimonides' position on the Oral Law are Kalman Kahana, *Heker ve-Iyun* (Tel Aviv: Mosad Yitzhak Breuer, 1960), pp. 7–37, and Gerald Blidstein's "Maimonides on Oral Law," *The Jewish Law Annual,* vol. 1 (Leiden: E. J. Brill, 1978), pp. 108–122.

7. Leviticus 23:40.

8. Ibid.

9. Maimonides, *Introduction* p. 83.

10. *Sifra* 12, 16:4; *Sukkah* 35a.

11. Laws belonging to this category are commonly referred to as *halakhot le-Moshe mi-Sinai.*

12. For a complete list of laws belonging to this group, see Maimonides, *Introduction,* pp. 85–87.

13. Ibid., pp. 88–90.

14. Cf. Moses Maimonides, *Sefer ha-Mitzvot,* ed. Hayyim Heller (Jerusalem: Mosad Harav Kook, 1946), pp. 7–8; *Mishneh Torah, Ishut 1:2.* The position followed here is according to Yitzhak De-Leon, *Megillat Esther, Sefer ha-Mitzvot le-Ranbam* (New York: Jacob Shurkin, 1955), *shoresh* 2, pp. 11–23.

15. *Sanhedrin* 74a.

16. *Menahot* 29b.

17. See the comment of Hayyim ibn Attar, *Or ha-Hayyim,* Leviticus 13:34.

18. Isaac Halevi, *Dorot ha-Rishonim,* vol. 4 (Jerusalem: Mekor, 1966), p. 487.

19. Maimonides, *Introduction,* pp. 90–92.

20. *Avot* 1:1.

21. Numbers 6:3–4.

22. For a fine elaboration on this theme, see Moshe Hayyim Luzzatto, *Mesilat Yesharim* (New York: Feldheim, 1980), chap. 13.

23. *Rosh Ha-Shanah* 29b.

24. Maimonides, *Mishneh Torah, Mammrim* 2:3.

25. *Mishnah Terumot* 8:4; *Tosafot, Avodah Zarah* 35a, s.v. *hadah.*

26. *Mishnah Rosh Ha-Shanah* 4:3.

27. *Bava Metzia* 86b.

28. *Pesahim* 50b.

29. *Yerushalmi Yevamot* 12:1; *Bava Metzia* 7:1.

30. Cf. Elon, *Jewish Law,* 2:733–739.

31. Joseph Kalir, "The Minhag," *Tradition* 7(1965):91.

32. Deuteronomy 4:2.

33. Maimonides, *Mishneh Torah, Mammrim* 2:9.

34. Ibid., p. 107.

35. William Foxwell Albright, *From the Stone Age to Christianity* (New York: Doubleday: Anchor, 1957), p. 64.

36. *Temurah* 14b.

37. Maimonides, *Mishneh Torah,* Introduction. See Saul Lieberman, *Hellenism in Jewish Palestine* (New York: Jewish Theological Seminary of America, 1962), pp. 83–99.

38. *Shemot Rabbah* 47:1.

CHAPTER 3

1. Sherira b. Hanina, *Iggeret R. Sherira Gaon,* ed. B. M. Lewin (Jerusalem: Mekor, 1971), p. 39; Jacob N. Epstein, *Introduction to Tannaitic Literature* (Jerusalem: Magnes-Dvir, 1957), pp. 501–505.

2. Adin Steinsaltz, *The Essential Talmud* (New York: Bantam Books, 1976), p. 15.

3. George Foot Moore, *Judaism in the First Centuries of the Christian Era,* vol. 1 (New York: Schocken, 1971), pp. 88–89.

4. See David Hoffmann, "le-Heker Midreshei ha-Tannaim," in *Mesilot le-Torat ha-Tannaim* (Tel Aviv, 1928), pp. 1–81.

5. The extant *Midreshei Halakhah* are: *Mekhilta* on Exodus, *Sifra* on Leviticus, and *Sifre* on Numbers and Deuteronomy.

6. Louis Finkelstein, *New Light From the Prophets* (New York: Basic Books, 1969), pp. 1–23.

7. *Mekhilta de-Rabbi Ishmael* trans. and ed. Jacob Lauterbach, vol. 2 (Philadelphia: Jewish Publication Society, 1933–1935), pp. 260–261.

8. The various theories have been collected by Benjamin De-Vries, *Mevo Kelali le-Sifrut ha-Talmudit* (Tel Aviv: Sinai, 1966), pp. 14–15.

9. Harry C. Schimmel, *The Oral Law* (New York: Feldheim, 1973), pp. 152–153.

10. See Hanokh Albeck, *Introduction to the Mishnah* (Tel Aviv: Bialik Institute, 1959), pp. 65–66; David Hoffmann, *The First Mishnah and the Controversies of the Tannaim* (New York: Maurosho Publications, 1977), pp. 19–64.

11. Ibid., pp. 82–87.

12. Moses Maimonides, *Mishneh Torah,* Introduction.

13. Rashi, *Shabbat* 13b, s.v. *megillat; Eruvin* 62b, s.v. *ke-gon; Bava Metzia* 33b, s.v. *be-yemei.*

14. See Albeck, *Introduction to the Mishnah,* pp. 270–283.

15. *Avot de-Rabbi Natan,* ed. Solomon Schechter (New York: Feldheim, 1967), chap. 18.

16. De-Vries, *Mevo Kelali le-Sifrut ha-Talmudit,* pp. 29–35; Schimmel, *Oral Law,* p. 146.

17. *Bava Metzia* 86a.

18. Steinsaltz, *Essential Talmud,* p. 40.

19. The four tractates not having *Tosefta* are *Avot, Tamid, Middot,* and *Kinhim.*

20. Cf. Hanokh Albeck, *Mehkarim be-Baraita ve-Tosefta* (Jerusalem: Mosad Harav Kook, 1944), pp. 139–184.

21. *Midrash Shir ha-Shirim* 6:14.

CHAPTER 4

1. See *Bava Metzia* 86a.

2. See chapter 3.

3. Cf. Hanokh Albeck, *Introduction to the Talmud* (Tel Aviv: Dvir Company, 1969), p. 7.

4. Moses Maimonides, *Introduction to the Commentary on the Mishnah,* p. 149.

5. Abraham Weiss, *Studies in the Literature of the Amoraim* (New York: Yeshiva University Press, 1962), p. 1.

6. Abraham Weiss, *Le-Heker ha-Talmud* (New York: Feldheim, 1954), p. 3.

7. Ibid., pp. 10–17.

8. *Kiddushin* 41a.

9. *Mishnah Kiddushin* 1:1.

10. Ibid., 2:1.

11. *Kiddushin* 41b.

12. Ibid., 41a.

13. Ibid.

14. Ibid.

15. Ibid.

16. *Mishnah Bava Kamma* 1:1.

17. Adin Steinsaltz, *The Essential Talmud* (New York: Bantam Books, 1976), p. 228.

18. Ibid., p. 229.

19. Ibid.

20. *Bava Metzia* 86a.

21. See Julius Kaplan, *The Redaction of the Babylonian Talmud* (New York: Bloch, 1933), pp. 3–27.

22. See Meyer S. Feldblum, "Professor Abraham Weiss: His Approach and Contributions to Talmudic Scholarship," in *The Abraham Weiss Jubilee Volume* (New York: Yeshiva University, 1964), pp. 43–49; Shamai Kanter, "Abraham Weiss: Source Criticism," in *The Formation of the Babylonian Talmud,* ed. Jacob Neusner (Leiden: E. J. Brill, 1970), pp. 91–94.

23. Sherira b. Hanina, *Iggret R. Sherira Gaon,* ed. B. M. Lewin (Jerusalem: Mekor, 1971), pp. 69–70.

24. Louis Ginzberg, *On Jewish Law and Lore* (Philadelphia: Jewish Publication Society, 1955), p. 25.

25. Michael Avi-Yonah, *The Jews of Palestine* (New York: Schocken, 1976), pp. 178–181.

26. Steinsaltz, *Essential Talmud,* p. 54.

27. See Isaac Alfasi, *Sefer ha-Halakhot,* end of *Eruvin; Shitah Mekubezet* ed. Bezalel Ashkenazi, *Bava Metzia,* 12a, s.v. *be-megureshet;* Yosef ibn Megas, *Responsa* no. 81. (Jerusalem: Chaim Gittler, 1959), p. 14a.

28. *Shitah Mekubezet, Bava Metzia,* 12a, s.v. *be-megureshet.*

29. Ginzberg, *On Jewish Law and Lore,* p. 38; Abraham Weiss, *Hithavut ha-Talmud Bishelemuto* (New York: Mosad Le-Zichron Alexander Kohut, 1943), pp. 129, 137–159.

30. Weiss, *Hithavut ha-Talmud Bishelemuto,* pp. 137–159.

31. See Raphael Rabbinovicz, *History of the Printing of the Talmud* (Jerusalem: Mosad Harav Kook, 1965), p. 7ff.

CHAPTER 5

1. Abraham Cohen, *Everyman's Talmud* (New York: Schocken, 1975), p. xxxiv.

2. See Shmuel ha-Nagid, *Mevo ha-Talmud;* Leopold Zunz, *Ha-Derashot be-Yisrael,* ed. H. Albeck (Jerusalem: Mosad Bialik, 1954), p. 250.

3. Moses Maimonides, *Introduction to the Commentary on the Mishnah,* pp. 150–151.

4. *Sotah* 40a.

5. Abraham Joshua Heschel, *God In Search of Man* (Philadelphia: Jewish Publication Society, 1956), p. 336.

6. Ibid., p. 344.

7. Jeremiah 23:29.

8. See *Shabbat* 88b and Rashi, Exodus 6:9.

9. Cohen, *Everyman's Talmud,* p. xxxv.

10. *Mishnah Shabbat* 6:4.

11. *Shabbat* 63a.

12. Ibid.

13. Ibid.

14. *Avot* 5:27.

15. Abraham ibn Ezra, *Ibn Ezra Al ha-Torah,* ed. A. Weiser, vol. 1 (Jerusalem: Mosad Harav Kook, 1976), p. 10.

16. Ibid.

17. Exodus 21:24.

18. *Bava Kamma* 84a.

19. See Samuel Belkin, *In His Image* (New York: Abelard-Schuman, 1960), pp. 41–43.

20. See Ovadiah b. Ya'akov Sforno, *Commentary on the Pentateuch,* Exodus 21:24.

21. Moses Maimonides, *The Guide of the Perplexed,* trans. Shlomo Pines, vol. 2 (Chicago: Chicago University Press, 1963), p. 573.

22. *Ketubbot* 75a, 111b; *Bava Batra* 73a–74b.

23. *Berakhot* 6a; *Rosh Ha-Shanah* 17b, *Avodah Zarah* 3b.

24. *Berakhot* 61b.

25. *Taanit* 21a, *Treatise Ta'anit of the Babylonian Talmud,* trans. and ed. Henry Malter (Philadelphia: Jewish Publication Society, 1967), pp. 304, 306.

26. Marc Saperstein, *Decoding the Rabbis* (Cambridge: Harvard University Press, 1980), p. 1.

27. Ibid., pp. 7–8.

28. Ibid., pp. 9–10.

29. *Pesahim* 54a.

30. Judah Halevi, *Book of Kuzari,* trans. Hartwig Hirschfeld (New York: Pardes, 1946), p. 173.

31. Maimonides, *Introduction to the Commentary on the Mishnah,* pp. 150–155.

32. See James Kugel, "Two Introductions to Midrash," *Prooftexts,* 3:2(1983):131–155.

CHAPTER 6

1. Moshe Silberg, *Talmudic Law and the Modern State* (New York: Burning Bush Press, 1973), p. 1.

2. Adin Steinsaltz, *The Essential Talmud* (New York: Bantam Books, 1976), p. 163.

3. *Berakhot* 19b.

4. *Bava Kamma* 27a; *Bava Batra* 92a.

5. *Tosafot, Shevuot* 30b, s.v. *aval.*

6. Ibid., *Bava Kamma* 27b, s.v. *ka-mashma lan.*

7. *Yevamot* 89b.

8. *Kiddushin* 41b.

9. Numbers 18:28.

10. *Kiddushin* 41a–41b.

11. Exodus 12:6.

12. *Kiddushin* 41b.

13. *Sanhedrin* 73a.

14. *Arakhin* 22a.

15. Silberg, *Talmudic Law,* p. 68.

16. *Arakhin* 22a.

17. For a fine exposition of this theme, see Ahron Soloveitchik, "Civil Rights in Terms of Halachah," *Viewpoint* (May 1964):1–7.

18. *Bava Metzia* 59b.

19. Exodus 23:2.

20. *Bava Metzia* 59b.

21. Cf. Saul Lieberman, *Greek in Jewish Palestine* (New York: Jewish Theological Seminary of America, 1965), p. 144, n. 2.

22. *Yerushalmi Rosh Ha-Shanah* 1:3, Lieberman, *Greek in Jewish Palestine,* pp. 37–38.

23. Genesis 1:27.

24. The bulk of these laws are discussed in *Mishnah* and *Gemara Makkot* and *Sanhedrin.*

25. *Mishnah Makkot* 1:10.

26. *Makkot* 7a.

27. Gerald Blidstein, "Capital Punishment—The Classic Jewish Discussion," in *Understanding the Talmud,* ed. Alan Corre (New York: Ktav, 1975), p. 319.

28. See Moshe Meiselman, "Capital Punishment in Jewish Law," *Gesher* 8:1(1981):23–35.

29. *Gittin* 10b; *Bava Kamma* 113a; *Bava Batra* 54b.

30. Leo Landman, *Jewish Law in the Diaspora* (Philadelphia: Dropsie University Press, 1968), p. 22.

31. See Menahem b. Shlomo ha-Meiri, *Bet ha-Behirah, Baba Kamma* 113a, s.v. *af.*

32. R. Nissim, *Nedarim* 28a. See also R. Shmuel b. Meir (Rashbam), *Bava Batra* 54b.

33. Moses Maimonides, *Mishneh Torah, Gezelah ve-Avedah* 5:11; *Zehiya u-Matanah* 1:15.

34. Aaron Rakefet-Rothkoff, "Dina D'Malkhuta Dina—The Law of the Land in Halakhic Perspective," *Tradition* 13:2(1972):16–21.

CHAPTER 7

1. Ecclesiasticus 38:24–34, 39:1–8.

2. Ibid., 39:8.

3. *Avot* 3:9.

4. Ibid., 6:5–6.

5. *Berakhot* 35b.

6. Ibid., 32b.

7. Ephraim E. Urbach, *The Sages,* vol. 1 (Jerusalem: Magnes Press, 1975), p. 608.

8. *Yerushalmi Megillah* 1:9.

9. See *Mishnah Taanit* 3:8.

10. See *Hullin* 110a; *Niddah* 25b, 36b; *Shabbat* 139a; *Eruvin* 44b, 74a.

11. *Taanit* 23a, 24a.

12. *Taanit* 20b.

13. Cf. *Yerushalmi Taanit* 4:2.

14. *Yerushalmi Kilayim* 9:3.

15. *Sifre* Deuteronomy 357:7.

16. *Pesahim* 66a.

17. *Yoma* 35b.

18. *Pesahim* 66a; *Yerushalmi Pesahim* 6:1.

19. *Avot* 1:13.

20. *Ketubbot* 67b.

21. *Avot* 1:12.

22. *Shabbat* 31a; see also Adolph Buchler, *Types of Jewish-*

Palestinian Piety from 70 B.C.E. to 70 C.E. (New York: Ktav, 1968), pp. 10–12.

23. *Shabbat* 31a.

24. Deuteronomy 15:1–2.

25. *Mishnah Sheviit* 10:3.

26. Ibid., 10:4.

27. *Gittin* 36a, Rashi s.v. *mosrani.*

28. See *Tosafot, Gittin* 36a, s.v. *mi ikha;* Harry Schimmel, *The Oral Law* (New York: Feldheim, 1973), pp. 127–129.

29. Concerning the name *Lakish* see Wilhelm Bacher, *Agadat Amorai Eretz Yisrael,* vol. 1 (Tel Aviv: Dvir Company, 1920), p. 130, n. 1.

30. *Gittin* 47a; *Yerushalmi Gittin* 4:9.

31. *Yerushalmi Moed Katan* 3:1.

32. *Bava Metzia* 84a.

33. Ibid.

34. *Sanhedrin* 24a.

35. *Shir ha-Shirim Rabbah* 1:6.

CHAPTER 8

1. Simhah Assaf, *Tekufat ha-Geonim ve-Sifrutah* (Jerusalem: Mosad Harav Kook, 1955), pp. 137–138.

2. Ibid., pp. 139–146.

3. Abraham ibn Daud, *The Book of Tradition (Sefer ha-Qabbalah),* trans. Gershon D. Cohen (Philadelphia: Jewish Publication Society, 1967), pp. 63–66.

4. Cf. Gershon D. Cohen, "The Story of the Four Captives," *Proceedings of the American Academy for Jewish Research* 29(1960–1961):55–131.

5. Cf. Solomon Luria, *Responsa,* no. 29 (New York: Menahem Wagshal, 1958), p. 23a.

6. Irving A. Agus, *The Heroic Age of Franco-German Jewry* (New York: Yeshiva University Press, 1969), pp. 1–6.

7. Irving A. Agus, "Rabbinic Scholarship in Northern Eu-

rope," in *The World History of the Jewish People: The Dark Ages,* ed. Cecil Roth (Ramat Gan: Rutgers University Press, 1966), p. 191.

8. Ibid., p. 195.

9. Ibid.

10. Esra Shereshevsky, *Rashi: The Man and His World* (New York: Sepher-Hermon Press, 1982), p. 140.

11. Menahem b. Zerah, *Tzedah la-Derekh* (Warsaw: Hayyim Kelter, 1880), Introduction.

12. See Ephraim E. Urbach, *The Tosaphists* (Jerusalem: Mosad Bialik, 1955).

13. Cf. H. J. Zimmels, "Scholars and Scholarship in Byzantium and Italy," in *The World History of the Jewish People: The Dark Ages,* ed. Cecil Roth (Ramat Gan: Rutgers University Press, 1960), pp. 182–184.

14. See Isadore Twersky, "Aspects of the Social and Cultural History of Provencal Jewry," in *Jewish Society Throughout the Ages,* ed. H. H. Ben Sasson and S. Ettinger (New York: Schocken, 1969), pp. 185–207.

15. Meyer Waxman, *A History of Jewish Literature,* vol. 2 (New York: Thomas Yoseloff, 1960), p. 115.

16. Adin Steinsaltz, *The Essential Talmud* (New York: Bantam Books, 1976), p. 245; Joseph B. Soloveitchik, *Divrei Hagot ve-Ha'arakha* (Jerusalem: World Zionist Organization, 1981), pp. 70–85.

17. See *Encyclopaedia Judaica,* ed. Cecil Roth, vol. 15 (Jerusalem: Keter Publishing House, 1974), p. 129; Norman Solomon, "Definition and Classification in the Works of the Lithuanian Halakhists," *Dine Israel* 6(1975):lxxiii–ciii.

CHAPTER 9

1. *Shemot Rabbah* 47:1.

2. See James Parkes, *The Conflict of the Church and the Synagogue* (New York: Meridian Books, 1964), p. 392.

3. Ibid.

4. Allan Temko, "The Burning of the Talmud," in *Understanding the Talmud,* ed. Allan Corre (New York: Ktav, 1975), p. 140.

5. Jacob R. Marcus, *The Jew in the Medieval World* (New York: Athenaeum, 1969), p. 167.

6. See *Encyclopaedia Judaica,* ed. Cecil Roth, vol. 4 (Jerusalem: Keter Publishing House, 1972), p. 400.

7. Temko, "Burning of the Talmud," in Corre, *Understanding the Talmud,* p. 138.

8. *Ozar Vikhuhim,* ed. J. D. Eisentein (New York, 1928), pp. 81–86.

9. See I. Loeb, "La Controverse de 1240 sur le Talmud," *Revue Des Etudes Juives,* 1(1880):247–261; 2(1881):248–270; 3(1882): 39–57.

10. Solomon Grayzel, *The Church and the Jews in the XIIIth Century* (Philadelphia: Dropsie University Press, 1933), pp. 238–243.

11. Marcus, *Jew in the Medieval World,* p. 146. Cf. Leon Poliakov, *The History of Anti-Semitism* (New York: Vanguard Press, 1965), p. 69.

12. See Robert Chazan, *Medieval Jewry in Northern France* (Baltimore: Johns Hopkins, 1973), p. 124, n. 79; Dudley Wright, *The Talmud* (London: William and Norgate, 1932), p. 111.

13. Grayzel, *Church and the Jews,* pp. 250–253.

14. *Ozar Vikhuhim,* p. 85.

15. Jacob Katz, *Exclusiveness and Tolerance* (New York: Schocken, 1962), p. 110.

16. Edward H. Flannery, *The Anguish of the Jews* (New York: Macmillan, 1965), p. 105.

17. Quoted in *Encyclopaedia Judaica* 14:109.

18. Ibid., 13:357. Concerning Erasmus's view of the Jews, see Heiko A. Oberman, "Three Sixteenth-Century Attitudes to Judaism: Reuchlin, Erasmus and Luther," in *Jewish Thought in the Sixteenth Century,* ed. Bernard Dov Cooperman (Cambridge: Harvard University Press, 1983), pp. 339–342.

19. *Yevamot* 63a.

20. See Raphael Rabbinovicz, *History of the Printing of the Talmud* (Jerusalem: Mosad Harav Kook, 1965), pp. 76–78.

21. Flannery, *Anguish of the Jews,* p. 105.

CHAPTER 10

1. Ephraim E. Urbach, *The Sages,* vol. 1 (Jerusalem: Magnes Press, 1975), p. 4.

2. Yitzhak Baer, *Israel Among the Nations* (Jerusalem: Schocken, 1955), pp. 81–98.

3. Saul Lieberman, "How Much Greek in Jewish Palestine?" in *Biblical and Other Studies,* ed. Alexander Altmann (Cambridge: Harvard University Press, 1963), pp. 127–132.

4. Ibid., p. 223.

5. Ibid., p. 220.

6. Baer, *Israel,* pp. 81–98.

7. See *Avot* 1:3, 4:12; *Tosefta Sotah* 14:4; *Tosefta Yoma* 2:8.

8. *Avot* 3:4; *Mishnah Eduyyot* 5:6; *Pirke de-Rabbi Eliezer* (Warsaw: xxx, 1852), chap. 35, p. 82a.

9. Joseph H. Hertz, *The Authorised Prayer Book* (New York: Bloch, 1954), pp. 130–134.

10. *Taanit* 23a.

11. *Avot* 3:1.

12. *Yerushalmi Berakhot* 9:1.

13. *Sifre* Numbers, sec. 84.

14. *Sanhedrin* 39a.

15. See *Eliyahu Rabbah* (Jerusalem: Levin-Epstein, 1961), chap. 18.

16. *Yoma* 38b.

17. *Hullin* 7b.

18. *Sotah* 2a.

19. *Ketubbot* 30a.

20. *Berakhot* 33b.

21. See *Avot* 3:15.

22. Steven T. Katz, *Jewish Ideas and Concepts* (New York: Schocken, 1977), pp. 121–122.

23. Moses Maimonides, *Mishnah Commentary, Avot* 3:15.

24. *Sifra, Kedoshim* 7:1.

25. Deuteronomy 13:5.

26. *Sotah* 14a.

27. *Avodah Zarah* 20b.

28. See *Avot* 3:2, 4:22; *Mishnah Makkot* 3:16.

29. *Sifra, Kedoshim* 7:1.

30. Exodus 19:6.

31. *Mekhilta de-Rabbi Ishmael,* ed. H. S. Horowitz and I. A. Rabin (Jerusalem: Bamberger and Wahrman, 1960), p. 209.

32. *Sifra, Kedoshim* 7:1.

33. *Mishnah Kelim* 1:6.

34. *Mishnah Megillah* 3:1.

35. *Berakhot* 55a.

36. See *Taanit* 11a, 22b.

37. Ibid., 11a.

38. Samuel N. Hoenig, *Talmudic Thought* (New York: American Jewish Committee, 1976), p. 53.

39. Menachem Marc Kellner, *Contemporary Jewish Ethics* (New York: Sanhedrin Press, 1979), p. 5.

40. *Mishnah Yoma* 8:9.

41. Leviticus 18:4.

42. *Yoma* 67b.

43. *Kiddushin* 31a.

44. See *Tosafot, Kiddushin* 31a, s.v. *gadol.*

45. *Mishnah Makkot* 3:16.

46. *Bava Batra* 8a.

47. *Peah* 1:1.

48. *Rosh Ha-Shanah* 6a.

49. *Bava Batra* 8b; *Ketubbot* 49b. Cf. Moses Maimonides, *Mishneh Torah, Matenot Aniyim* 7:10, *Tosafot, Ketubot* 49b, s.v. *akfiye.*

50. *Avot de-Rabbi Natan,* ed. Solomon Schechter (New York: Feldheim, 1967b), p. 57.

51. Isadore Twersky, "Some Aspects of the Jewish Attitude Toward the Welfare State," *Tradition* 5:2(1963):144–145.

52. See Horowitz and Rabin, *Mekhilta de-Rabbi Ishmael,* p. 245; *Avot* 3:14.

53. *Bava Metzia* 58b.

54. *Mishnah Bava Kamma* 8:1.

55. *Shabbat* 94b.

56. Exodus 20:26.

57. Horowitz and Rabin, *Mekhilta de-Rabbi Ishmael,* p. 245. See Ahron Soloveitchik, "Civil Rights in Terms of Halachah," *Viewpoint* (May 1964):1–7.

58. Exodus 18:20.

59. *Bava Metzia* 30b.

60. Ibid.

61. Ibid., 24b.

62. Ibid., 83a.

63. Adin Steinsaltz, *The Essential Talmud* (New York: Bantam Books, 1976), p. 201.

64. *Yerushalmi Terumot* 8:4; *Bereshit Rabbah,* sec. 94, pp. 1184–1185.

65. *Tosefta Terumot* 7:20.

66. David Daube, *Collaboration With Tyranny In Rabbinic Law* (London: Oxford University, 1965), p. 12.

67. *Bereshit Rabbah,* sec. 94, pp. 1184–1185.

68. Aharon Lichtenstein, "Does Jewish Tradition Recognize an Ethic Independent of Halakha?" in *Modern Jewish Ethics,* ed. Marvin Fox (Columbus, OH: Ohio State University Press, 1975), p. 83.

69. *Mishnah Bava Kamma* 6:4.

70. Ibid.

71. *Mishnah Bava Metzia* 3:3.

72. Ibid., 2:11.

73. *Bava Metzia* 33a.

74. Ibid., 62a.

75. See Hoenig, *Talmudic Thought,* p. 58.

76. Irving M. Bunim, *Ethics From Sinai,* vol. 1 (New York: Feldheim, 1964), p. xviii.

77. Hertz, *Authorised Prayer Book,* p. 611.

78. *Bava Kamma* 30a.

79. Erich Fromm, *You Shall Be As Gods* (New York: Fawcett, 1966), pp. 44–45.

80. Jacob Neusner, "The Tasks of Theology in Judaism: A Humanistic Program," *The Journal of Religion* 59:1(1979):78.

81. David S. Shapiro, *Studies in Jewish Thought* (New York: Yeshiva University Press, 1975), p. 124.

82. *Sifre* Numbers, sec. 112.

83. Shapiro, *Studies,* p. 131.

84. *Yerushalmi Kiddushin* 4:12.

85. *Tanhuma,* ed. S. Buber, vol. 2 (Jerusalem, 1964), p. 30.

86. Joseph B. Soloveitchik, "Catharsis," *Tradition* 17:2(1978): 38.

87. *Avot* 4:17.

88. See *Yoma* 85a; *Sanhedrin* 74a.

89. *Tanhuma,* 2:161–162.

90. Exodus 20:8.

91. Ibid., 20:10.

92. *Mishnah Shabbat* 7:2.

93. *Sanhedrin* 62b.

94. I. Grunfeld, *The Sabbath* (New York: Feldheim, 1959), p. 28.

95. Erich Fromm, *To Have Or To Be?* (New York: Bantam Books, 1981), p. 40.

96. *Pesikta Rabbati,* ed. M. Friedman (Vienna: Meir Friedman, 1880), p. 121a.

97. *Betzah* 16a.

98. *Shabbat* 12b.

99. Fromm, *To Have Or To Be?,* p. 40.

100. *Tosefta Berakhot* 3:7.

101. *Kiddushin* 40b.

102. *Avot* 2:6.

103. *Shabbat* 10a.

104. Ibid.

105. *Avot* 6:1.

106. Jeremiah 33:25.

107. *Pesahim* 78b.

108. *Sanhedrin* 99b.

109. Shapiro, *Studies,* p. 136.

110. *Berakhot* 64a. For an outstanding and penetrating study of the halakhic way, see Joseph B. Soloveitchik, *Halakhic Man,* trans. L. Kaplan (Philadelphia: Jewish Publication Society, 1983). Also see Zerah Warhaftig, "The Relevance and Dynamics of Halakhah," *Contemporary Thinking in Israel* 1(1973):90–120.

CHAPTER 11

1. Abraham Joshua Heschel, *The Earth Is the Lord's* (Cleveland and New York: The World Publishing Company; Philadelphia: Jewish Publication Society, 1963), p. 47.

2. Ibid., p. 46.

3. Ibid.

4. Ibid., p. 50.

5. William B. Helmreich, *The World of the Yeshiva* (New York: Free Press, 1982), p. 7.

6. See Joseph Litvin, "Naphtali Tzevi Berlin," in *Men of the Spirit,* ed. Leo Jung (New York: Kymson Publishing Company, 1964), pp. 287–299.

7. See Gedalyahu Alon, "The Lithuanian Yeshivas," in *The Jewish Expression,* ed. Judah Goldin (New York: Bantam Books, 1970), pp. 448–464.

8. Cf. Isadore Twersky, *Introduction to the Code of Maimonides (Mishnah Torah)* (New Haven: Yale University Press, 1980), pp. 238–323, "The Shulhan 'Aruk: Enduring Code of Jewish Law," in *The Jewish Expression,* ed. Judah Goldin (New York: Bantam Books, 1970), pp. 322–343.

9. Cf. Moshe Meiselman, *Jewish Woman in Jewish Law* (New York: Ktav, 1978), pp. 73–115.

10. Cf. Fred Rosner, "The Jewish Attitude Toward Euthanasia," in *Jewish Bioethics,* ed. Fred Rosner and J. David Bleich (New York: Sanhedrin Press, 1979), pp. 253–265.

11. Cf. Gerald Blidstein, "Capital Punishment—The Classic Jewish Discussion," in *Understanding the Talmud,* ed. Alan Corre (New York: Ktav, 1975), pp. 313–324; Moshe Meiselman, "Capital Punishment in Jewish Law," *Gesher* 8:1(1981):23–35.

12. J. David Bleich, "Abortion in Halakhic Literature," in *Jewish Bioethics,* pp. 134–177.

13. Norman Lamm, "The Religious Implications of Extraterrestrial Life," *Tradition* 7:4(1966):5–56.

14. Azriel Rosenfeld, "Judaism and Gene Design," in *Jewish Bioethics,* pp. 401–408; Fred Rosner, "Test Tube Babies, Host Mothers and Genetic Engineering in Judaism," *Tradition* 19(1981):141–148.

15. Adin Steinsaltz, *The Essential Talmud* (New York: Bantam Books, 1976), p. 267.

16. Irving A. Agus, *The Heroic Age of Franco-German Jewry* (New York: Yeshiva University Press, 1969), pp. 7–9.

17. See Irving J. Rosenbaum, *The Holocaust and Halakhah* (New York: Ktav, 1976), pp. 54–55.

18. Ibid.

19. See Hayyim Nahman Bialik, *Kol Kitvei Hayyim Nahman Bialik* (Tel Aviv: Dvir Company, 1954), pp. 17–18. The English text quoted here is based on the translation of Philip M. Raskin, *Collected Poems of Philip M. Raskin* (New York: Bloch Publishing Company, 1951), pp. 113–114.

20. Steinsaltz, *Essential Talmud,* p. 269.

21. Ibid.

22. Joseph B. Soloveitchik, "On the Love of Torah: Impromptu Remarks at a Siyyum," in *Shiurei ha-Rav,* ed. Joseph Epstein (New York: Hamevaser, Yeshiva University Press, 1974), p. 104.

GLOSSARY

Aggadah (pl. -*dot*)—homiletical and ethical portion of ancient rabbinical literature, legends, and parables contained in the Talmud.

Amora (pl. -*im*)—"expounders," the sages whose teachings were eventually compiled in the Talmud.

Anshe Keneset ha-Gedolah—"Men of the Great Assembly"; sometimes called *sofrim*.

Av Bet-Din—Father of the Court

Avot—"the fathers"; refers to the tractate Ethics of the Fathers.

Bakashah—petition.

Baraita (pl. -*tot*)—"outside teaching," i.e., outside the canon of the *Mishnah*.

Dina de-Malkhuta Dina—"the law of the kingdom is the law."

Derash—deriving law by creative interpretation of the biblical text.

Eretz Yisrael—the land of Israel.

195

Etrog—a citron; one of the "four kinds" used in the ceremony of the harvest festival of Sukkot.

Gemara—"completion" or "finished work"; popular name for the Talmud.

Geonim—the heads of the Babylonian academies in the posttalmudic era.

Gezerah (pl. *rot*)—"decrees."

Hakhamim—"sages"; usually refers to talmudic sages.

Halakhah—Jewish law.

Ha-Makom—the Omnipresent.

Hatraah—"sounding the alarm"; warning to be given by a witness to a person about to commit a capital crime.

Hazakah—presumptive title established by prior practice.

Hefker—ownerless property.

Hiluk—the dialectic method of studying Talmud; see *Pilpul* below.

Horaah—"instruction"; teaching leading to the final redaction of the Talmud.

Issurai—laws concerning ritual or ceremonial practice.

Kal va-Homer—making an inference from a major to a minor or a minor to a major premise.

Kavod ha-Briyot—"respect for God's creatures"; especially the principle of human dignity.

Kedushah—holiness.

Kedushat ha-Makom—holiness of place.

Kedushat ha-Zeman—holiness of time.

Lifnim mishurat ha-din—"beyond the strict law."

Lulav—palm branch.

Mamonot—laws of civil and monetary character.

Massekhtot—tractates.

Mehilah—waiver.

Melakhah—work.

Memra (pl. *-rot*)—"a saying"; refers to a short amoraic statement that contains a complete idea without any dialectics.

Midrash (pl. *-im*)—refers to the searching out of the meaning of the Pentateuch.

Minhag—custom.

Mishnah—compilation of the Oral Law made at the close of the second century.

Mishnat hasidim—the teaching of the pious.

Mishnayot—smaller units into which chapters of the *Mishnah* are divided.

Mitzvah (pl. *-vot*)—"commandments."

Nasi—president or head of the Sanhedrin.

Nefashot—concerning capital law.

Nehutei—"those who go down"; the emissaries who went abroad from Palestine to raise funds for their academies.

Peshat—the plain meaning of the text.

Perishut—separation from that which is not holy.

Pilpul—the dialectic method of studying Talmud.

Prosbol—a document in which the creditor declares that he has handed over his debt to the court for collection.

Resh Galuta—the Exilarch.

Rosh yeshivah—the head of the academy.

Saboraim—the teachers of the Talmud in the two centuries following the compilation of the Babylonian Talmud and leading to its final editing.

Sedarim—"orders," such as the six orders of the *Mishnah.*

Shamayim—heaven.

Shehitah—ritual slaughter of animals.

Shema—literally "hear"; the prayer calling upon the people of Israel to affirm the Oneness of God.

Shishah Sedarim—the six orders of the *Mishnah,* sometimes abbreviated as *Shas.*

Sugyah (pl. *-yot*)—the treatment of a single topic in a dialectical form.

Takanah (pl. *-not*)—ordinances.

Talmid hakham—scholar.

Talmud—the name given to the compilation of the teachings and commentaries of the Oral Law.

Talmud Bavli—the Babylonian Talmud.

Talmud Yerushalmi—The Jerusalem or Palestinian Talmud.

Tanakh—the acronym for the Hebrew designation of the three main sections of the Jewish Bible—*Torah* (the Five Books of Moses); *Nevi'im* (Prophets); *Ketuvim* (Writings).

Tanna (pl. *-im*)—a teacher of the first and second centuries in the land of Israel.

Tefillin—phylacteries.

Torah—the Law; also the Five Books of Moses.

Torah lishmah—the study of Torah for its own sake.

Torah Min ha-Shamayim—Torah from heaven; revealed law.

Torah she-Ba-al Peh—the Oral Law.

Torah she-Bekhtav—the Written Law.

Tosefta—a collection of tannaitic teachings written in the mishnaic style.

Yarhei Kallah—months set aside for convocations to study Talmud.

Yeshivah (pl. *-vot*)—seat of academic learning.

Zekanim—elders.

Zugot—"pairs"; refers to the two heads of the Sanhedrin.

BIBLIOGRAPHY

Agus, Irving A. "Rabbinic Scholarship in Northern Europe." In *The World History of the Jewish People: The Dark Ages,* edited by Cecil Roth, pp. 189–209. Ramat Gan: Rutgers University Press, 1966.
_____ . *The Heroic Age of Franco-German Jewry.* New York: Yeshiva University Press, 1969.
Albeck, Hanokh. *Mehkarim be-Baraita ve-Tosefta.* Jerusalem: Mosad Harav Kook, 1944.
_____ . *Introduction to the Mishnah.* Tel Aviv: Bialik Institute, 1959.
_____ . *Introduction to the Talmud.* Tel Aviv: Dvir Company, 1969.
Albright, William Foxwell. *From the Stone Age to Christianity.* New York: Doubleday–Anchor, 1957.
Alfasi, Isaac. *Sefer ha-Halakhot.* Standard editions of the Babylonian Talmud. New York: Otzar Hasefarim, 1965.
Alon, Gedalyahu. "The Lithuanian Yeshivas." In *The Jewish Expression,* edited by Judah Goldin, pp. 448–464. New York: Bantam Books, 1970.
Assaf, Simhah. *Tekufat ha-Geonim ve-Sifrutah.* Jerusalem: Mosad Harav Kook, 1955.
Avi-Yonah, Michael. *The Jews of Palestine.* New York: Schocken, 1976.

Avot de-Rabbi Natan. Edited by Solomon Schechter. New York: Feldheim, 1967. Translated by Judah Goldin, *The Fathers According to Rabbi Nathan.* New Haven: Yale University Press, 1955.

Bacher, Wilhelm. *Agadat Amorai Eretz Yisrael.* Tel Aviv: Dvir Company, 1920.

Baer, Yitzhak. *Israel Among the Nations.* Jerusalem: Schocken, 1955.

Belkin, Samuel. *In His Image.* New York: Abelard-Schuman, 1960.

Bialik, Hayyim Nahman. *Kol Kitvei Hayyim Nahman Bialik.* Tel Aviv: Dvir Company, 1954.

Bleich, J. David. "Abortion in Halakhic Literature." In *Jewish Bioethics,* edited by Fred Rosner and J. David Bleich, pp. 134–177. New York: Sanhedrin Press, 1979.

Blidstein, Gerald. "Capital Punishment—The Classic Jewish Discussion." In *Understanding the Talmud,* edited by Alan Corre, pp. 313–324. New York: Ktav, 1975.

————. "Maimonides on Oral Law." In *The Jewish Law Annual,* vol. 1, pp. 108–122. Leiden: E. J. Brill, 1978.

Buchler, Adolph. *Types of Jewish-Palestinian Piety from 70 B.C.E. to 70 C.E.* New York: Ktav, 1968.

Bunim, Irving M. *Ethics From Sinai (An Eclectic, Wide Ranging Commentary on Pirke Avot).* 3 vols. New York: Feldheim, 1964.

Chazan, Robert. *Medieval Jewry in Northern France.* Baltimore: Johns Hopkins, 1973.

Cohen, Abraham. *Everyman's Talmud.* New York: Schocken, 1975.

Cohen, Gerson D. "The Story of the Four Captives." *Proceedings of the American Academy for Jewish Research* 29 (1960–1961):55–131.

Daube, David. *Collaboration With Tyranny In Rabbinic Law.* London: Oxford University, 1965.

De-Leon, Yitzhak. *Megillat Esther, Sefer ha-Mitzvot le-Rambam.* New York: Jacob Shurkin, 1955.

De-Vries, Benjamin. *Mevo Kelali le-Sifrut ha-Talmudit.* Tel Aviv: Sinai, 1966.

Drazin, Nathan. *History of Jewish Education From 515 B.C.E. To 220 C.E.* Baltimore: Johns Hopkins, 1940.

Dupont-Sommer, A. *The Essene Writings From Qumran.* Oxford: Oxford University, 1961.

Eliyahu Rabbah (Sefer Tanna de-Bei Eliyahu). Jerusalem: Levin-Epstein, 1961.

Elon, Menahem. *Jewish Law.* 3 vols. Jerusalem: Magnes, 1973.

Encyclopaedia Judaica. 15 vols. Edited by Cecil Roth. Jerusalem: Keter Publishing House, 1972.

Encyclopedia Talmudit. Edited by Shlomo Yosef Zevin. Jerusalem: World Mizrachi Organization, 1959.

Ephrathi, Jacob E. *The Sevoraic Period and Its Literature.* Petah Tikvah: Agudath Bnai Asher, 1973.

Epstein, Jacob N. *Introduction to Tannaitic Literature.* Jerusalem: Magnes-Dvir, 1957.

Feldblum, Meyer S. "Professor Abraham Weiss: His Approach and Contributions to Talmudic Scholarship." In *The Abraham Weiss Jubilee Volume,* pp. 7–80. New York: Yeshiva University, 1964.

Finkelstein, Louis. *New Light From the Prophets.* New York: Basic Books, 1969.

Flannery, Edward H. *The Anguish Of The Jews.* New York: Macmillan, 1965.

Fromm, Erich. *You Shall Be As Gods.* New York: Fawcett, 1966.

_____ . *To Have Or To Be?* New York: Bantam Books, 1981.

Ginzberg, Louis. *On Jewish Law and Lore.* Philadelphia: Jewish Publication Society, 1955.

Grayzel, Solomon. *The Church and the Jews in the XIIIth Century.* Philadelphia: Dropsie University Press, 1933.

Grunfeld, I. *The Sabbath.* New York: Feldheim, 1959.

Gutkowski, J. *The Era of the Second Temple* (A New Edition of *Korot Am Olam*). New York: Shengold, 1974.

Guttmann, Alexander. *Rabbinic Judaism in the Making.* Detroit: Wayne State University Press, 1970.

Halevi, Isaac. *Dorot ha-Rishonim.* 5 vols. Jerusalem: Mekor, 1966.

Halevi, Judah. *Book of Kuzari.* Translated from the Arabic by Hartwig Hirschfeld. New York: Pardes, 1946.

Helmreich, William B. *The World of the Yeshiva.* New York: Free Press, 1982.

Hertz, Joseph H. *The Authorised Prayer Book.* New York: Bloch, 1954.

Heschel, Abraham Joshua. *The Earth Is The Lord's.* Cleveland and New York: The World Publishing Company; Philadelphia: Jewish Publication Society, 1963.

———— . *God In Search of Man.* Philadelphia: Jewish Publication Society, 1956.

Hirsch, Samson Raphael. *The Pentateuch.* Translated and explained by Samson R. Hirsch. 6 vols. Gateshead: Judaica Press, 1973.

Hoenig, Samuel N. *Talmudic Thought.* New York: American Jewish Committee, 1976.

Hoenig, Sidney B. *The Great Sanhedrin.* Philadelphia: Dropsie University Press, 1953.

———— . "Pre-Karaism and the Sectarian (Qumran) Scrolls." In *Joshua Finkel Festschrift,* pp. 71–94. New York: Yeshiva University Press, 1973.

———— . "Qumran Fantasies." *The Jewish Quarterly Review* 63:4(1973):247–268; 292–317.

Hoffmann, David. "le-Heker Midreshei ha-Tannaim." In *Mesilot le-Torat ha-Tannaim.* Tel Aviv, 1928.

———— . *The First Mishnah and the Controversies of the Tannaim.* New York: Maurosho Publications, 1977.

Ibn Attar, Hayyim. *Or ha-Hayyim.* Printed in various editions of the Rabbinic Bible *(Mikraot Gedolot).* New York: Shulsinger Brothers, 1950–1978.

Ibn Daud, Abraham. *The Book of Tradition (Sefer ha-Qabbalah).* Translated and annotated by Gerson D. Cohen. Philadelphia: Jewish Publication Society, 1967.

Ibn Ezra, Abraham. *Ibn Ezra Al ha-Torah.* Edited by A. Weiser. Jerusalem: Mosad Harav Kook, 1976.

Ibn Megas, Yosef. *Responsa.* Jerusalem: Chaim Gittler, 1959.

Josephus. *Complete Works of Flavius Josephus.* Translated by William Whiston. Grand Rapids: Kregel Publications, 1971.

Kahana, Kalman. *Heker ve-Iyun.* Tel Aviv: Mosad Yitzhak Breuer, 1960.

Kalir, Joseph. "The Minhag." *Tradition* 7:2(1965):89–95.

Kanter, Shamai. "Abraham Weiss: Source Criticism." *The Formation of the Babylonian Talmud,* edited by Jacob Neusner, pp. 87–94. Leiden: E. J. Brill, 1970.

Kaplan, Julius. *The Redaction of the Babylonian Talmud.* New York: Bloch, 1933.

Katz, Jacob. *Exclusiveness and Tolerance.* New York: Schocken, 1962.

Katz, Steven T. *Jewish Ideas and Concepts.* New York: Schocken, 1977.

Kellner, Menachem Marc. *Contemporary Jewish Ethics.* New York: Sanhedrin Press, 1979.

Kugel, James. "Two Introductions to Midrash." *Prooftexts* 3:2(1983): 131–155.

Lamm, Norman. "The Religious Implications of Extraterrestrial Life." *Tradition* 7:4(1966):5–56.

Landman, Leo. *Jewish Law in the Diaspora: Confrontation and Accommodation.* Philadelphia: Dropsie University Press, 1968.

Lichtenstein, Aharon. "Does Jewish Tradition Recognize an Ethic Independent of Halakhah?" In *Modern Jewish Ethics,* edited by Marvin Fox, pp. 62–88. Columbus, OH: Ohio State University Press, 1975.

Lieberman, Saul. *Hellenism in Jewish Palestine.* New York: Jewish Theological Seminary of America, 1962.

_____ . "How Much Greek in Jewish Palestine?" In *Biblical and Other Studies,* edited by Alexander Altmann, pp. 123–141. Cambridge: Harvard University Press, 1963.

_____ . *Greek in Jewish Palestine.* New York: Jewish Theological Seminary of America, 1965.

Litvin, Joseph. "Naphtali Tzevi Berlin (The Netziv)." In *Men of the Spirit,* edited by Leo Jung, pp. 287–299. New York: Krymson Publishing Company, 1964.

Loeb, I. "La Controverse de 1240 sur le Talmud." *Revue Des Etudes Juives* 1(1880):247–261; 2(1881):248–270; 3(1882):39–57.

Luria, Solomon. *Responsa.* New York: Menahem Wagshal, 1958.

Luzzatto, Moshe Hayyim. *Mesilat Yesharim.* New York: Feldheim, 1980.

Maimonides, Moses. *Sefer ha-Mitzvot.* Edited by Hayyim Heller. Jerusalem: Mosad Harav Kook, 1946.

_____ . *Mishneh Torah.* Standard edition with commentaries. Vilna: Abraham Zvi Rosenkranz, 1900.

_____ . *The Guide of the Perplexed.* 2 vols. Translated by Shlomo Pines. Chicago: Chicago University Press, 1963.

_____ . *Introduction to the Commentary on the Mishnah.* Translated and annotated by Zvi L. Lampel under the tile *Maimonides' Introduction to the Talmud.* New York: Judaica Press, 1975.

Marcus, Jacob R. *The Jew in the Medieval World.* New York: Athenaeum, 1969.

Medieval Jewish Chronicles and Chronological Notes. 2 vols. Edited by A.
Neubauer. Oxford: Clarendon Press, 1895.

Meiselman, Moshe. *Jewish Woman in Jewish Law.* New York: Ktav,
1978.

————. "Capital Punishment in Jewish Law." *Gesher* 8:1(1981):
23–35.

Mekhilta de-Rabbi Ishmael. 3 vols. Translated and edited by Jacob
Lauterbach. Philadelphia: Jewish Publication Society,
1933–1935.

Mekhilta de-Rabbi Ishmael. Edited by H. S. Horowitz and I. A. Rabin.
Jerusalem: Bamberger and Wahrman, 1960.

Menahem b. Shlomo ha-Meiri. *Bet ha-Behirah, Baba Kamma.* Jerusalem: Mosad Harav Kook, 1950.

Menahem b. Zerah. *Tzedah la-Derekh.* Warsaw: Hayyim Kelter,
1880.

Midrash Bereshit Rabbah. 3 vols. Edited by J. Theodor and H. Albeck.
Jerusalem: Wahrman Books, 1965.

Midrash Rabbah. Standard edition with commentaries. 2 vols. Jerusalem: Fisher Publications, 1982.

Mirsky, Samuel K. "The Formation of the Mishnah and the Babylonian Talmud." In *Tractate Endings of the Mishnah and the Babylonian Talmud.* New York: Young Israel Synagogue of Boro Park,
1961.

Mishnah. 6 vols. Edited by H. Albeck. Tel Aviv: Bialik-Dvir, 1958.

Moore, George Foot. *Judaism in the First Centuries of the Christian Era.*
2 vols. New York: Schocken, 1971.

Neusner, Jacob. *There We Sat Down.* Nashville: Abingdon Press,
1972.

————. "The Tasks of Theology in Judaism: A Humanistic Program." *The Journal of Religion* 59:1(1979):71–86.

Oberman, Heiko A. "Three Sixteenth-Century Attitudes to Judaism: Reuchlin, Erasmus and Luther." In *Jewish Thought in the
Sixteenth Century,* edited by Bernard Dov Cooperman, pp.
326–364. Cambridge: Harvard University Press, 1983.

Ozar Vikhuhim. Edited by J. D. Eisenstein. New York, 1928.

Parkes, James. *The Conflict of the Church and the Synagogue.* New
York: Meridian Books, 1964.

Pirkei de-Rabbi Eliezer. Warsaw: Shmuel Eliezer Luria, 1852.

Pesikta Rabbati. Edited by M. Friedman. Vienna: Meir Friedman, 1880.

Poliakov, Leon. *The History of Anti-Semitism.* New York: Vanguard Press, 1965.

Rabbinovicz, Raphael. *History of the Printing of the Talmud.* Jerusalem: Mosad Harav Kook, 1965.

Rakefet-Rothkoff, Aaron. "Dina D'Malkhuta Dina—The Law of the Land in Halakhic Perspective." *Tradition* 13:2(1972):5–23.

Rosenbaum, Irving J. *The Holocaust and Halakhah.* New York: Ktav, 1976.

Rosenfeld, Azriel. "Judaism and Gene Design." In *Jewish Bioethics,* edited by Fred Rosner and J. David Bleich, pp. 401–408. New York: Sanhedrin Press, 1979.

Rosner, Fred. "The Jewish Attitude Toward Euthanasia." In *Jewish Bioethics,* edited by Fred Rosner and J. David Bleich, pp. 253–265. New York: Sanhedrin Press, 1979.

————. "Test Tube Babies, Host Mothers and Genetic Engineering in Judaism." *Tradition* 19(1981):141–148.

Rotenberg, Shlomo. *Toldot Am Olam.* Vol. 1. Jerusalem: Keren Eliezer, 1967.

Saperstein, Marc. *Decoding the Rabbis: A Thirteenth-Century Commentary on the Aggadah.* Cambridge: Harvard University Press, 1980.

Schechter, Solomon. *Studies in Judaism.* 3rd ser. Philadelphia: Jewish Publication Society, 1924.

Schimmel, Harry C. *The Oral Law: A Study of the Rabbinic Contribution to Torah She-Be-Al Peh.* New York: Feldheim, 1973.

Sforno, Ovadiah b. Yaakov. *Commentary on the Pentateuch.* Printed in various editions of the Rabbinic Bible *(Mikraot Gedolot).* New York: Shulsinger Brothers, 1950–1978.

Shapiro, David. *Studies in Jewish Thought.* New York: Yeshiva University Press, 1975.

Shereshevsky, Esra. *Rashi: The Man and His World.* New York: Sepher-Hermon Press, 1982.

Sherira b. Hanina. *Iggeret R. Sherira Gaon.* Edited by B. M. Lewin. Jerusalem: Mekor, 1971.

Shitah Mekubezet. Anthology of commentaries on select tractates of the Babylonian Talmud. Edited by Bezalel Ashkenazi. New York: Feldheim, 1952.

Shmuel ha-Nagid. *Mevo ha-Talmud.* Standard editions of Babylonian Talmud (end of tractate *Berakhot*). New York: Otzar Hasefarim, 1965.

Sifra. Jerusalem: Sifrah Publishers, 1959.

Sifre Numbers and Sifre Zuta. Edited by H. S. Horowitz. Jerusalem: Wahrman Books, 1966.

Sifre Deuteronomy. Edited by Louis Finkelstein. New York: Jewish Theological Seminary of America, 1969.

Silberg, Moshe. *Talmudic Law and the Modern State.* New York: Burning Bush Press, 1973.

Sirach. The Apocrypha and Pseudepigrapha of the Old Testament in English, vol. 1, edited by R. H. Charles, pp. 316–517. London: Oxford University Press, 1913.

Solomon b. Isaac of Troyes (Rashi). *Commentary on the Talmud.* Printed in all standard editions of the Babylonian Talmud. New York: Otzar Hasefarim, 1965.

_____ . *Perushei Rashi Al ha-Torah* (Commentary on the Pentateuch). Edited by C. D. Chavel. Jerusalem: Mosad Harav Kook, 1983.

Solomon, Norman. "Definition and Classification in the Works of the Lithuanian Halakhists." *Dine Israel* 6(1975):lxxiii–ciii.

Soloveitchik, Ahron. "Civil Rights in Terms of Halachah." *Viewpoint,* May 1964, 1–7.

Soloveitchik, Joseph B. "On the Love of Torah: Impromtu Remarks at a Siyyum." In *Shiurei ha-Rav,* edited by Joseph Epstein, pp. 102–104. New York: Hamevaser, Yeshiva University Press, 1974.

_____ . "Catharsis." *Tradition* 17:2(1978):38–54.

_____ . *Divrei Hagot ve-Ha'arakha.* Jerusalem: World Zionist Organization, 1981.

_____ . *Halakhic Man.* Translated from the Hebrew by Lawrence Kaplan. Philadelphia: Jewish Publication Society, 1983.

Steinsaltz, Adin. *The Essential Talmud.* New York: Bantam Books, 1976.

Talmud, Babylonian. Standard edition. New York: Otzar Hasefarim, 1965.

Talmud, Yerushalmi (Palestinian). New York: Gilead Press, 1949.

Tanhuma. 2 vols. Edited by S. Buber. Jerusalem, 1964.

Temko, Allan. "The Burning of the Talmud." In *Understanding the Talmud,* edited by Allan Corre, pp. 124–140. New York: Ktav, 1975.

Tosafot. Printed in all editions of the Babylonian Talmud. New York: Otzar Hasefarim, 1965.

Tosefta. Edited by M. S. Zukermandel. Jerusalem: Wahrman Books, 1963.

Treatise Ta'anit of the Babylonian Talmud. Translated and edited by Henry Malter. Philadelphia: Jewish Publication Society, 1967.

Twersky, Isadore. "Some Aspects of the Jewish Attitude Toward the Welfare State." *Tradition* 5:2(1963):137–158.

————. "Aspects of the Social and Cultural History of Provencal Jewry." In *Jewish Society Throughout the Ages,* edited by H. H. Ben Sasson and S. Ettinger, pp. 185–207. New York: Schocken, 1969.

————. "The Shulhan 'Aruk: Enduring Code of Jewish Law." In *The Jewish Expression,* edited by Judah Goldin, pp. 322–343. New York: Bantam Books, 1970.

————. *Introduction to the Code of Maimonides (Mishneh Torah).* New Haven: Yale University Press, 1980.

Urbach, Ephraim E. *The Tosaphists: Their History, Writings and Methods.* Jerusalem: Mosad Bialik, 1955.

————. *The Sages: Their Concepts and Beliefs.* 2 vols. Jerusalem: Magnes Press, 1975.

Warhaftig, Zerah. "The Relevance and Dynamics of Halakhah." *Contemporary Thinking in Israel* 1(1973):90–120.

Waxman, Meyer. *A History of Jewish Literature.* 6 vols. New York: Thomas Yoseloff, 1960.

Weiss, Abraham. *Hithavut ha-Talmud Bishelemuto.* New York: Mosad Le-Zichron Alexander Kohut, 1943.

————. *Le-Heker ha-Talmud.* New York: Feldheim, 1954.

————. *Studies in the Literature of the Amoraim.* New York: Yeshiva University Press, 1962.

Wright, Dudley. *The Talmud.* London: Williams and Norgate, 1932.

Yadin, Yigael. *The Message of the Scrolls.* New York: Simon and Schuster, 1957.

Zeitlin, Solomon. "An Historical Study of the Canonization of the Hebrew Scriptures." In *The Canon and Masorah of the Hebrew Bible,* edited by Sid Z. Leiman, pp. 164–199. New York: Ktav, 1974.

Zimmels, H. J. "Scholars and Scholarship in Byzantium and Italy."
    In *The World History of the Jewish People: The Dark Ages,* edited by
    Cecil Roth, pp. 175–188. Ramat Gan: Rutgers University Press,
    1960.
Zunz, Leopold. *Ha-Derashot be-Yisrael.* Edited and annotated by H.
    Albeck. Jerusalem: Mosad Bialik, 1954.

INDEX

About the Author

Rabbi Samuel N. Hoenig holds a Ph.D. in Talmudic Studies from Yeshiva University, where he also obtained his master's degree in Jewish History and his bachelor's degree in Hebrew Language and Literature. He received his rabbinic ordination from Rabbi Isaac Elchanan Theological Seminary. Rabbi Hoenig's association with Touro College began in 1973, and he presently teaches in both its liberal arts and graduate schools. He has published in both English and Hebrew on talmudic thought, the halakhic code, responsa literature, and Jewish history and education.